ORGAN HARVESTING: AN EXAMINATION OF A BRUTAL PRACTICE

JOINT HEARING

BEFORE THE

SUBCOMMITTEE ON AFRICA, GLOBAL HEALTH, GLOBAL HUMAN RIGHTS, AND INTERNATIONAL ORGANIZATIONS

AND THE

SUBCOMMITTEE ON EUROPE, EURASIA, AND EMERGING THREATS

OF THE

COMMITTEE ON FOREIGN AFFAIRS
HOUSE OF REPRESENTATIVES

ONE HUNDRED FOURTEENTH CONGRESS

SECOND SESSION

JUNE 23, 2016

Serial No. 114–170

Printed for the use of the Committee on Foreign Affairs

Available via the World Wide Web: http://www.foreignaffairs.house.gov/ or http://www.gpo.gov/fdsys/

U.S. GOVERNMENT PUBLISHING OFFICE

20–533PDF   WASHINGTON : 2016

For sale by the Superintendent of Documents, U.S. Government Publishing Office
Internet: bookstore.gpo.gov   Phone: toll free (866) 512–1800; DC area (202) 512–1800
Fax: (202) 512–2104   Mail: Stop IDCC, Washington, DC 20402–0001

(II)

CONTENTS

ORGAN HARVESTING: AN EXAMINATION OF A BRUTAL PRACTICE

THURSDAY, JUNE 23, 2016

House of Representatives,
Subcommittee on Africa, Global Health,
Global Human Rights, and International Organizations and
Subcommittee on Europe, Eurasia, and Emerging Threats,
Committee on Foreign Affairs,
Washington, DC.

The subcommittee met, pursuant to notice, at 2 o'clock p.m., in room 2200 Rayburn House Office Building, Hon. Dana T. Rohrabacher (chairman of the Subcommittee on Europe, Eurasia, and Emerging Threats) presiding.

Mr. ROHRABACHER. I call this joint hearing of the Europe, Eurasia, and Emerging Threats Subcommittee and the Subcommittee on Africa, Global Health, Global Human Rights, and International Organizations to order.

Thank you, Chairman Smith, for agreeing to hold this hearing. The Chinese Communist Party has one of the largest forces for evil in the world today. The systematic government-sponsored harvesting of organs is a monstrous crime.

The Chinese regime not only deprives its people of their basic rights on a daily basis but literally steals their body parts for a profit.

Due to the tireless work of human rights defenders, journalists and investigators, the truth about what the Chinese have been doing for years is now becoming known to the world.

Just last week, the House passed a resolution specifically on this target. Today, we have some of those very researchers and investigators here with us and they will bring up to date about what is going on inside China.

Their updated report, ''Bloody Harvest: The Slaughter,'' just released yesterday tips the scale at nearly 600 pages in length and it is truly an impressive work.

I am pleased to hear that European parliaments will be holding similar events to what we are doing today to discuss organ harvesting and this report.

It is significant to highlight that while the Falun Gong practitioners, a peaceful and holy Chinese movement, continue to suffer greatly at the hands of the CCP, they are not the only victims of forced organ harvesting.

Organ harvesting is just one of many techniques the Chinese state security uses. But there are other groups who use this and other groups that have been victimized other than just the Falun Gong.

Lastly, the problem of organ theft and organ trafficking is a global one. The state-sponsored nature of what happens in China is especially unsavory but the practice takes place worldwide.

The black market for organs is estimated to be worth over $1 billion a year and it is vital that we hold the Chinese Government accountable. If we don't, the wrong message will be sent all over the world, undermining efforts to prevent organ trafficking where it is done.

In a moment, I will introduce our witnesses. But I also want to take this moment to recognize some of the distinguished guests in our audience and especially David Kilgour, who is a member of the Canadian Parliament.

We have been working on this together for many years. He is a true leader in this issue and a truly moral giant in this era. He has played a key role in producing the updated report and David, we all thank you for the hard work that you put into this.

And without objection, all members will have 5 legislative days to submit additional questions or extraneous material. We will then—I will have—Mr. Smith will make his opening remarks and then we will introduce the witnesses and go on from there.

Mr. Smith.

Mr. SMITH. Thank you very much. I would like to say to my dear friend and colleague, Dana Rohrabacher, for organizing this important hearing.

There are far too few people willing to speak out about human rights abuses with such clarity and consistency. As a former speechwriter for President Ronald Reagan, Dana Rohrabacher knows how to cut right to the heart of the matter.

He has done so with excellence since I have been here in Congress. I have been now serving 36 years as a Member. So I want to thank him for his extraordinary leadership on human rights issues around the world and including and especially in China.

As Chairman Rohrabacher mentioned, we co-chaired a similar hearing in September 2012. It is disheartening in the extreme that we are here again, 4 years later, with the issue and this terrible horrific human rights abuse getting worse.

The scope of organ trafficking is much larger now, a worldwide problem. The conflict in Syria has created a black market for human organs. ISIS has sanctioned the harvesting and sale of organs from a ''apostate's body into a Muslim's body'' even if the donor is still alive during harvesting.

We have also seen horrific evidence of Eritrean victims in Sinai whose organs are brutally removed and sold if their families are unable to pay the traffickers' ransom.

However, the biggest problem is, by far, China, where government-sanctioned harvesting of organs from executed prisoners, including prisoners of conscience, has gone on for decades.

Twenty years ago, working with the great and now late Harry Wu, I chaired a human rights hearing in my subcommittee with a Chinese security official who testified that he and other security agents were executing prisoners with doctors and ambulances there in order to steal their organs for transplant.

Since then, this horrific practice has skyrocketed. Organ trafficking is a global problem where trafficking gangs, terrorist organizations, and government entities sell organs for profit. A global problem requires a global response.

The U.S. Congress is taking steps to address the problem. The House passed H.R. 3694, two weeks ago, the Strategy To Oppose Predatory Organ Trafficking Act, amending the Trafficking Victims Protection Act of 2000 and requiring more diplomatic action in reporting on the issue. The bill also denies visas to doctors and officials complicit in organ trafficking.

This is a start, and it is only a start, and hopefully the Senate will pass the bill soon.

Four years ago, we asked for more evidence of organ harvesting in China and we are now getting some very serious evidence. The Chinese Government said it is moving toward adherence to ethical standards and accepted procedural guidelines.

But in the absence of accurate information and any semblance of transparency and with a history of repression and censorship to cover past abuses can their assurances be in any way believed?

It is important to remember that the Chinese Government has been trafficking in organs for profit for decades. Let me just say many things have changed in China over the past 20 years, but as witness testimony today shows, maybe not so much as changed in the area of organ harvesting.

The Falun Gong repression is especially brutal, ugly, and vicious. I strongly believe that the 17-year campaign to eradicate Falun Gong will be seen as one of the great shames of recent Chinese history.

That more people are not crying out for change, accountability and justice on the issue of organ harvesting or the repression of the Falun Gong is sad. But that has to change, too. This hearing helps to bring these issues into sharp light and to bring scrutiny to them.

What adjectives do we use to describe what Chinese doctors and hospitals have been doing these past decades? How can we describe doctors who engage in forced abortions and sterilizations and gendercide, the extermination of the girl child, as we have seen in China?

How can we understand doctors who experiment on prisoners of conscience detained in psychiatric hospitals? It is all reminiscent of what happened during World War II in some of the camps including Camp 731 when people were horrifically abused, in that case by Chinese conquerors in China. And now the Chinese Government and the doctors are doing it themselves.

Ordinary words like concerned, disturbed, or shocking just don't seem to be adequate. We tend to reserve words like barbaric for truly horrible crimes and this is barbaric.

The Department of State and the international medical community must do a detailed analysis and studies on the claims made by respected researchers here today and by Falun Gong practitioners. Our State Department has done far too little. That, too, has to change.

I yield back and I thank my friend for calling this hearing.

Mr. ROHRABACHER. Thank you very much, Chris, and I would like to now introduce our witnesses.

David Matas is an international human rights lawyer based in Canada. He has written extensively on organ harvesting in China including co-authoring "Bloody Harvest" with David Kilgour, who I just mentioned. He is one of the co-authors of the updated report and we will be hearing more about that in just a moment.

Also, Ethan Gutmann, who is—is it Gutmann or Gutmann? Whichever. You know, like Rohrabacher—they say how do you pronounce Rohrabacher.

As a China analyst and a human rights investigatory, he has written widely on China including the book "Losing the New China: The Story of American Commerce, Desire and Betrayal." He is a former policy analyst at the Brookings Institute and is a frequent television news commentator.

We have with us Dr. Francis Delmonico, who is a professor of surgery at Harvard Medical School and chief medical officer for the New England Organ Bank and an advisor to the World Health Organization.

He is also immediate past president of the Transplantation Society, the leading international association for professionals who are involved with the transplantation of human organs and tissues.

Finally, we have Dr. Charles Lee. He is the director of public awareness for the World Organization to Investigate the Persecution of the Falun Gong.

He received his medical education in China and later came to the United States where he passed the U.S. Medical Board exams and during a visit to China in 2003 he was arrested and sentenced to 3 years in prison.

Since his return to the United States in 2006, he has continued his work to expose the crimes of the CCP, especially those crimes against the Falun Gong.

I would ask each of you if possible to limit your verbal remarks to 5 minutes and then to have whatever extraneous material or supporting material to be put into the record and they will be automatically done—will be automatically put into the record.

So Dr. Matas, you may proceed.

STATEMENT OF MR. DAVID MATAS, SENIOR LEGAL COUNSEL, B'NAI BRITH CANADA

Mr. MATAS. Yes. Well, first of all, I want to thank the two committees for convening this hearing and I want to commend the co-chairs, Representatives Smith and Rohrabacher, for their—your leadership in this issue.

David Kilgour, who is behind me, and I have been researching, writing and speaking on the killing of Falun Gong for their organs now for over 10 years.

Ethan Gutmann is the journalist who interviewed us on our work and then did his own. Since David Kilgour and I published "Blood Harvest," the third version of our report in book form and Ethan Gutmann published his book, "The Slaughter," we three have remained active in writing, researching, investigating and speaking on organ transplant abuse in China.

Yesterday at the National Press Club, we released a 600-page update with over 2,300 footnotes to update this work and it is now available online at endorganpillaging.org.

With the update, we make our own assessment of transplant abuses and our own assessment of transplant volumes. In looking at the sources for organ transplants from China in the past we have taken Chinese Government official statements of overall transplant volume to 10,000 a year at face value and focused on attempting to identify the sources for these asserted volumes.

However, the Chinese Government statistics for transplant volumes are not necessarily reliable. One effort which needed to be made and which we find we have made is to determine on our own what Chinese transplant volumes are.

We did that by looking at and accumulating the data from individual hospitals where transplants occur, almost 900 in all. Some hospitals state their transplant volumes. For those who do not, we can from their bed counts, personnel strength, the rate of growth, technological development, academic publications, newsletters, media reports and so on come to a conclusion on their transplant volumes.

We had in the past concluded that the Chinese Communist Party was engaged in the mass killing of innocents, primarily practitioners of the spiritually-based set of exercises Falun Gong but also Uyghurs, Tibetans and select House Christians in order to obtain organs for transplants.

The fact that the evidence we have now examined shows a much larger volume of transplants than the Government of China has assured us points us to a larger discrepancy between transplant volumes and the Government of China identified sources than we had previously thought existed.

The increased discrepancy leads us to conclude there has been a far larger slaughter of practitioners of Falun Gong for their organs than we had originally estimated.

What is the volume of organ transplantation in China now when we add up all the data from the transplant centers and hospitals? Instead of 10,000 a year, we would say that the range is between 60,000 to 100,000 transplants a year with an emphasis on the higher number. The update at great length indicates how we calculate that range.

Well, what is to be done? We have to commend the House of Representatives for what they have already done, which you have referred to, Mr. Chairs—the stop organ trafficking act proposal as well as the resolution condemning a week ago the practice of state-sanctioned organ harvesting in the People's Republic of China.

We welcome the provision in the U.S. code which bars provision of visas to Chinese—other nationals engaged in coerced organ or bodily tissue transplantation.

Yet, there is more that could be done. Organ transplant abuse in China is primarily a donor source problem, not a supply problem, not a patient demand problem. We could end transplant tourism into China entirely and organ transplant abuse in China would still continue. Yet, we must do what we can to avoid complicity in that abuse.

House Resolution 343 calls on the United States Department of State to conduct a detailed analysis on state-sanctioned organ harvesting from nonconsenting prisoners of conscience in the annual human rights report.

I would suggest that this analysis must be more than just a presentation of the work that we and other researchers have done coupled with empty Chinese Government denials.

The Department of State Bureau of Human Rights to fulfil the mandate given by the House should come to its own conclusions.

There also needs to be a more direct confrontation of transplant tourism. U.S. legislation should make organ transplant abuse and brokerage extraterritorial crimes.

The legislation should require compulsory medical and hospital reporting of all out of country transplantation. That sort of reporting is necessary to make a law against complicity and foreign transplant abuse workable. Insurers should be prevented from covering and paying for abusive transplantation abroad.

Pharmaceutical companies should not be allowed to participate in drug trials with patients using organs from improper sources.

In conclusion, let me say when it comes to abusive transplantation, we have to think not only of the patient in need of an organ but also the source of the organ. It is unconscionable to kill a healthy innocent person so that a sick person can live. The U.S. must do everything in its power to stop that from happening.

Thank you very much.

[The prepared statement of Mr. Matas follows:]

Submission to a joint subcommittee hearing
Committee on Foreign Affairs
House of Representatives
US Congress
Washington DC
23 June, 2016

by David Matas

David Kilgour and I have been researching, writing, and speaking on the killing of Falun Gong for their organs now for ten years. Ethan Gutmann is a journalist who interviewed us on our work and then did his own.

Since David Kilgour and I published *Bloody Harvest,* the third version of our report in book form, and Ethan Gutmann published his book *The Slaughter,* we three have remained active in writing, researching, investigating and speaking on organ transplant abuse in China. Yesterday, at the National Press Club, we released an 817 page update to our work. It is now available on line.

This update undertook seven different tasks. One was to make our own assessment of transplant volumes. In looking at the sources for organ transplants in China, we have, in the past, taken Chinese government official statements of overall transplant volumes at face value and focused on attempting to identify the sources for those asserted volumes. However, Chinese government statistics for transplant volumes are not necessarily reliable. One effort which needed to be made and which we finally have made is to determine on our own what Chinese transplant volumes are.

We did that by looking at and accumulating the data from the individual hospitals where transplants occur. Some hospitals state their transplant volumes. For those who do not, we can, from their bed counts, personnel strength, potential patient groups, rate of growth, technological development, academic publications, and media reports, come to a conclusion on their transplant volumes.

A second task we undertook, flowing from the first, was addressing cover-up. Cover-up is a standard reaction to wrongdoing. Chinese Communist Party coverup is not a new story. But, because we are dealing new data, we consequently have to address cover up anew, attempts to hide individual hospital transplant figures.

Deception in the data limits the yield of research from that data. Because of the Chinese corruption of the data with which we are working, we cannot make specific numerical conclusions with complete certainty. Accordingly, our estimates of Chinese transplant volumes are not expressed in single integers but in a numerical range.

Despite the cover up and corruption of data, despite our inability to produce an exact figure, we are convinced that transplant volume is substantially higher than the official figure. The high volume led us into a third component of this update, to explore the driving factors behind these volumes.

Once we started looking at what is generating the volume, we had to look at the extent to which the Chinese Communist Party is in the driver's seat, the structure the regime has built around organ harvesting, and the culpability of some individual Party members. The update accordingly addresses that topic as well.

Fifth, we analyzed the Party's claims of recent transplant reform. The Chinese regime announces changes regularly on organ transplant sourcing, some of which are real, while some are not. Because the Party has moved since our last published works, we too have to move, to assess their claims of change and attempt to determine how real those claims are.

A sixth new feature of tour new work was incorporation of whistleblower evidence. In the past, we have tended to avoid reproducing that evidence, even though we had it. We have to protect the identities of whistleblowers. That protection, while understandable, means that an independent researcher cannot identify and question the whistleblowers him or herself.

Whistleblower evidence nonetheless deserves to be presented publicly, albeit with the identities of the whistleblowers disguised, if for no other reason than to encourage other whistleblowers to come forward. So it was presented in the update.

Finally, the update addressed plastination, in addition to organ sourcing, a subject we have mostly not addressed before. In the past, we have shied away from addressing plastination, because plastination is different from our focus, organ transplantation. Nonetheless, there is compelling evidence that practitioners of Falun Gong are killed for both plastination and organ sourcing. The evidence supporting each abuse is also evidence in support of the other abuse.

No one in the West has witnessed organ transplant abuse in China; yet a large number have seen plastinated bodies from China on display. Furthermore, plastinated body parts from China have been sold to medical schools and universities throughout the Western world. Plastination gives an immediate, widespread, publicly visible reality to the abuse that the killing of innocents for their organs cannot.

The ultimate conclusion of the update is that the Chinese Communist Party has engaged the State in the mass killings of innocents, primarily practitioners of the spiritually-based set of exercises, Falun Gong, but also Uyghurs, Tibetans, and select House Christians, in order to obtain organs for transplants.

Even with the volumes of transplants the Chinese government has asserted in the past, there is a substantial discrepancy between the number of transplants and the number of sources which the Government of China has identified - prisoners sentenced to death and voluntary donors. This discrepancy is one reason, among several, that had led us in the past to the conclusion that the above groups have been the source of many, and indeed most, organs for transplants.

The fact that the evidence we have now examined shows much larger volumes of transplants than the Government of China has asserted points to a larger discrepancy between transplant volumes and Government of China-identified sources than we had previously thought existed. That increased discrepancy leads us to conclude that there has been a far larger slaughter of practitioners of Falun Gong for their organs than we had originally estimated.

When we look at hospitals and doctors one by one, a number of features jump out. One is the sheer volume of transplants. The total number of transplants which officials ascribe to the country as a whole, ten thousand a year, is easily surpassed by just a few hospitals. Whatever the total number is, it must be substantially more, by a multiple, than the official figure.

Second, many of the hospitals are relatively new or have new transplant wings or beds. This development would not have occurred without confidence in a continuing supply of organs for transplants. The transplant business in China has developed with not only an abundance of available organs from 2001 on, but also with a confidence that this abundance would continue into the indefinite future.

Third, concomitant with the large number of transplants, there is a large number of qualified staff. The transplant industry in China employs a lot of people. The investment in people as well as buildings is another testimonial to the ready availability of high volumes of organs available for transplants, not only in the immediate past and present, but also, in the view of those who have committed their careers and the careers of others to this profession, into the indefinite future.

Fourth, the transplant professionals in China are engaged in substantial training and research. Research and training in transplants cannot be done without transplants. The high volume of research bespeaks itself a high volume of transplants and a ready availability of organs for transplants.

Fifth, the combination of a large professional corps, a substantial building stock and significant research speaks money. Transplantation in China means money, lots of it.

What is the volume when we add in all transplant centres and hospitals? We would say that the range is between 60,000 to 100,000 transplants a year, with an emphasis on the higher numbers. The update indicates how we calculate that range.

Well what is to be done? We have to commend the House of Representatives for what they have already done, both the resolution adopting the "Strategy To Oppose Predatory Organ Trafficking Act or the "STOP Organ Trafficking Act" as well as the resolution condemning the practice of state-sanctioned forced organ harvesting in the People's Republic of China. We welcome the provision of the United States Code which bars provision of visas to Chinese and other nationals engaged in coerced organ or bodily tissue transplantation. Yet, there is more that could be done.

Organ transplant abuse in China is primarily a donor source problem, a supply problem, not a patient or demand problem. We could end transplant tourism into China entirely and organ transplant abuse in China could still continue. Yet, we must do what we can to avoid complicity in that abuse.

House resolution 343 calls on the United States Department of State to conduct a detailed analysis on state sanctioned organ harvesting from non-consenting prisoners of conscience in the annual Human Rights Report. I would suggest that this analysis must be more than just a presentation of the work that we and other researchers have done coupled with empty Chinese government denials. The Department of State Bureau of Human Rights, to fulfil the mandate given by the House, should come to its own conclusions.

Let me present an historical analogy, by referring back to a different issue - slavery, a different country - Belgium, a different century - the early twentieth, and a different person - Edmund Morel, a shipping line clerk.

Edmund Morel came to the conclusion that King Leopold was engaged in slavery in the Congo from looking at shipments of goods between the Congo and Belgium. The goods to the Congo were guns, ammunition and explosives, which went to the state or its agents; no commercial goods were sent. The goods from the Congo were ivory and rubber, of much higher value than the goods sent. The locals were not allowed to use money. Edmund Morel asked, how were the ivory and rubber which were shipped to Belgium being purchased in the Congo? The answer, he concluded in research published first in 1901, was that they were not; the people producing the ivory and rubber were not being paid. They were slaves.

The conclusion was noteworthy because it was made without any eye witness evidence of slavery. It came just from shipping records. His work was initially met with official denials. Yet it was accurate.

Many people at the time were worried about offending Belgium by pressing the issue. The British Government nonetheless commissioned their consul in the Congo, Roger Casement, to conduct an independent investigation and write a report, which he did in 1904. Casement travelled throughout the Congo for three months and came back with a report which established the existence of slavery in the Congo beyond shadow of a doubt, despite, it should be said, the continuing denials of King Leopold of Belgium.

Today there is as much of a discrepancy today between the volume of transplants in China and sources of organs the Government of China is prepared to admit - death penalty prisoners and voluntary organs - as there was in the early twentieth century between the commercial value of goods being shipped into Congo and the commercial value of goods being shipped back to Belgium. The China discrepancy today points as much to a human rights violation as the Belgium discrepancy did yesterday. The need for an independent investigation is as great.

Perhaps David Kilgour, Ethan Gutmann and I can be cast in the role of Edmund Morel. But it is the Department of State Human Rights Bureau, with the mandate given to it by the House of Representatives, which should do what Roger Casement did, engage in an official investigation and produce a report.

There also needs to be more direct confrontation of transplant tourism. US legislation should make organ transplant abuse and brokerage extraterritorial crimes. The legislation should require compulsory medical and hospital reporting of all out of country transplantation. That sort of reporting is necessary to make a law against complicity in foreign transplant abuse workable. Insurers should be prevented from covering and paying for abusive transplantation abroad. Pharmaceutical companies should not be allowed to participate in drug trials with patients using organs from improper sources.

When it comes to abusive transplantation, we have to think not only of the patient in need of an organ, but also the source of the organ. It is unconscionable to kill a healthy person so that a sick person can live. The US must do everything in its power to stop that from happening.

....

David Matas is an international human rights lawyer based in Winnipeg, Manitoba, Canada.

Mr. ROHRABACHER. Thank you, sir.

Mr. Gutmann.

STATEMENT OF MR. ETHAN GUTMANN, JOURNALIST

Mr. GUTMANN. Thank you.

Fourteen years ago, the chairman of AmCham China gave testimony on Chinese intellectual property rights violations to the CECC. He testified the Chinese leadership was finally saying exactly what we wanted them to.

Yet, for U.S. companies selling to the Chinese market, 15 to 20 percent of revenue is lost due to counterfeiting. In other words, the problem was worse than ever.

That was Chris Murck. He is my former boss. He taught me that reform in China can take time. Eight years later, Murck came back to the CECC and testified that counterfeiting was present but it was receding and perhaps that is why when I was writing my book 7 years after the Kilgour-Matas report I assumed I was writing about history.

How naive. After decades of Western legal exchanges with China, Chinese lawyers now face mass arrests. How strangely idealistic the words free the Chinese Internet sound today in part because we know some American companies have dirty hands.

So yes, if money is the main issue, you might scratch out a stalemate with the Chinese Communist Party. But if the party feels threatened, take all the time you like. You will probably lose.

Our update is essentially a balance sheet of organ harvesting. Are we winning or losing? The Chinese medical establishment commonly claims that China performs 10,000 transplants per year.

Yet imagine a typical state-licensed transplant center in China. Three or four transplant teams, 30 or 40 beds for transplant patients, a 20- to 30-day recovery period. Patient demand—300 Chinese waitlisted for organs, not counting foreign organ tourists.

Would it be plausible to suggest that such a facility might do one transplant a day? One hundred and forty-six transplant facilities ministry-approved meet that general description. That yields a back of the envelope answer. You can do it right here. Not 10,000 but over 50,000 transplants per year.

Suppose we actually hold those same hospitals and transplant centers to the actual state minimum requirement of transplant activity, beds, surgical staff and so on—80,000 to 90,000 transplants per year.

Yet, how should we account for the emergency of Tianjin First Central Hospital, easily capable of 5,000 transplants per year? PLA 309 Military Hospital in Beijing, similar. Zhongshan Hospital—the list is extraordinary. A detailed examination yields an average of up to two transplants per day—over 100,000 transplants per year.

Now, the figures I have given you are based on Chinese numbers. Not from official statements but sources like Nurses Weekly.

To understand why organs are readily available we need to briefly examine how harvesting evolved over time. In the 1980s, it was an opportunistic afterthought to a convict's execution.

In the mid-1990s, medical vans on execution grounds became routine. Experimental live organ harvests were carried out on the execution grounds of Xinjiang.

In 1997, following the Ghulja massacre, a handful of political prisoners, Uyghur activists were harvested for a handful of aging Chinese Communist Party cadres.

Now, perhaps those organs were simply prizes seized in the fog of war. Perhaps the harvesting of prisoners of conscience could have ended there.

But in 1999, state security launched the campaign to eliminate Falun Gong. By 2001, over 1 million Falun Gong incarcerated within the Laogai system were subject to retail organ testing and Chinese military and civilian hospitals were ramping up their transplant facilities. By 2002, it was select House Christians. By 2003, it was the Tibetans.

By 2005, economic opportunism had been replaced by two hidden hands—5-year plan capitalism and the party's desire to kill off its internal enemies. The result was that a foreign organ tourist of means could purchase a tissue-matched organ within 2 weeks. Hardened criminals were harvested for organs; transplant centers stood to make $60,000, $100,000 or more but the rise of the Chinese transplant industry was built on the foundation of Falun Gong incarceration.

In early 2006, the Kilgour-Matas report was published and then we get into the business with Wang Lijun and the fatal exposure of the Chinese medical establishment.

In 2012, they promised to move to voluntary sourcing within 3 to 5 years. Yet, they wrapped it in a semantic trick. The phrase ''end organ harvesting of prisoners'' was acceptable. The phrase ''end organ harvesting of prisoners of conscience'' was unacceptable.

Thus, the Chinese could avoid speaking about a vast caught captive population that doesn't officially exist while the acceptable phrase allowed Westerners to hope that prisoners of conscience was just a subset of prisoners.

By avoiding the taboo phrase, both sides could maintain their illusions. Yet, throughout all the gyrations of the Chinese medical establishment's supposed reform, the inconsistent numbers, the dithering over whether a prisoner could volunteer their organs, the claim that a voluntary organ donation system was magically in place, our update finds only continuity. Transplant wings under construction, business as usual.

Now, in conclusion, as I turn to policy, let me begin with what can't be done. We cannot solve this problem by pretending that prisoners of conscience have not been harvested.

A Chinese doctor testified to Congress on the harvesting of death row prisoners in 2001 from Harry Wu. It caused a ripple, not a wave. We are here today, side by side, because the people in this room are concerned about prisoners of conscience.

We cannot verify self-proclaimed medical reform by arranged visits to a few Chinese transplant hospitals. In the words of Dr. Jacob Levee from the TTS ethics committee and Doctors Against Forced Organ Harvesting: ''As the son of a Holocaust survivor I feel obliged to not repeat the dreadful mistake made by the International Red Cross visit to the Theresienstadt Nazi concentration camp in 1944 in which it was reported to be a pleasant recreation camp.''

In short, the medical community cannot solve this problem alone. They need House Resolution 343. They need our research. And they need new investigations. They need to have oversight over Americans going to China for organs and they need the support of the American people.

According to Levee, not a single Israeli has gone to China for a transplant since Israel took a stand against organ tourism in 2008. Cutting off HMO funding wasn't enough.

The Israeli surgeons needed to make the point publically that no matter how much Chinese money was invested in Israeli software, doctors have a special interest in the phrase ''never again.''

Now, for Taiwan rejecting organ tourism to China was even more courageous, given the Chinese military threat. But if the Taiwanese medical establishment and the political sector can join hands, we can too.

I have been told that this is a Falun Gong issue. No. This is the familiar spectre of human genocide. It is cloaked in modern scrubs. And even with the united effort we may lose the patient. Yet, let us at least enter the operating room with clean hands.

Thank you.

[The prepared statement of Mr. Gutmann follows:]

Ethan Gutmann, author of *The Slaughter*

Committee on Foreign Affairs Hearing: Subcommittee on Africa, Global Health, Global Human Rights, and International Organizations, and the Subcommittee on Europe, Eurasia, and Emerging Threats

2:00 pm, June 23, 2016 in Room 2200, Rayburn House Office Building: "Organ Harvesting: An Examination of a Brutal Practice"

Fourteen years ago, the Chairman of the American Chamber of Commerce (AmCham) in China gave testimony on Chinese intellectual property rights violations to the Congressional Executive Commission on China (CECC). He testified that the Chinese leadership was finally saying exactly what we wanted them to. Yet for US companies selling to the Chinese market, "15-20% of revenue is lost due to counterfeiting." In other words, the problem was worse than ever.

That was Chris Murck, my former boss. He taught me that reform in China can take time. Eight years later Murck came back to the CECC and testified that counterfeiting was present, but receding. Perhaps that's why when I was writing my book, seven years after the Kilgour-Matas report, I assumed I was writing about history.

How naive. After decades of Western legal exchanges with China, Chinese lawyers face mass arrests. And how strangely idealistic the words "free the Chinese Internet" sound today—in part because we know some American companies have dirty hands. So yes, if money is the main issue, you might scratch out a stalemate with the Chinese Communist Party. But if the Party feels threatened, take all the time you like. You will probably lose.

Our Update is essentially a balance sheet of organ harvesting: Are we winning or losing?

The Chinese medical establishment commonly claims that China performs 10,000 transplants per year. Yet imagine a typical state-licensed transplant center in China: three or four transplant teams. 30 or 40 beds for transplant patients. A 20 to 30-day recovery period. Patient demand: 300,000 Chinese wait-listed for organs, not counting foreign organ tourists.

Would it be plausible to suggest that such a facility might do one transplant a day? 146 transplant facilities, ministry-approved, meet that general description. And that yields a back-of-the-envelope answer: not 10,000, but 50-60,000 transplants per year.

Suppose we actually hold those same hospitals and transplant centers to the actual state minimum requirement of transplant activity, beds, surgical staff, and so on? 80-90,000 transplants per year.

Yet how shall we account for the emergence of Tianjin First Central Hospital, easily capable of 5000 transplants per year? PLA 309 military hospital in Beijing? Zhongshan Hospital? The list is extraordinary. A detailed examination yields an average of up to two transplants a day, over 100,000 transplants a year.

Now the figures that I have just given you are based on Chinese numbers. Not from official statements, but sources like *Nurses Weekly*.

To understand why organs are readily available we need to examine how harvesting evolved over time. In the 1980s, it was an opportunistic afterthought to a convict's execution. In the mid-1990s, medical vans on execution grounds became routine and experimental live organ harvests were carried out on the execution grounds of Xinjiang. In 1997, following the Ghulja massacre, a handful of political prisoners, Uyghur activists, were harvested for a handful of aging Chinese Communist Party cadres.

Perhaps those organs were simply prizes seized in the fog of war. Perhaps the harvesting of prisoners of conscience could have ended there. But in 1999, State Security launched the campaign to eliminate Falun Gong. By 2001, over one million Falun Gong incarcerated within the Laogai System were subject to retail-organ testing, and Chinese military and civilian hospitals were ramping up their transplant facilities. By 2002, it was select House Christians. By 2003, it was the Tibetans' turn.

By 2005, economic opportunism had been replaced by two hidden hands—five-year-plan capitalism and the Party's desire to kill off its internal enemies. The result was that a foreign organ tourist of means could purchase a tissue-matched organ within two weeks. Hardened criminals were harvested for organs; transplant centers stood to make 60k, 100k, or more. But the rise of the Chinese transplant industry was built on the foundation of Falun Gong incarceration.

In early 2006, the Kilgour-Matas report was published. Beijing conceded that they used prisoner organs, ostensibly banned foreign organ tourism to China, and provided prisoners with permission-to-donate forms. In 2012, this thin tissue was shredded by the revelation that Bo Xilai's protege, Wang Lijun, ran a live organ harvesting center which had performed thousands of transplants.

Fatally exposed, the Chinese medical establishment promised to move to voluntary sourcing within 3-5 years, but wrapped it in a semantic trick: The phrase "end organ harvesting of prisoners" was acceptable. The phrase "end organ harvesting of prisoners of conscience" was unacceptable. Thus the Chinese could avoid speaking about a vast captive population that doesn't officially exist, while the acceptable phrase allowed Westerners to hope that "prisoners of conscience" was just a subset of "prisoners". By avoiding the taboo phrase, both sides could maintain their illusions.

Yet throughout all the gyrations of the Chinese medical establishment's supposed reform—the inconsistent numbers, the dithering over whether a prisoner could volunteer their organs, the claim that a voluntary donation system was magically in place—our Update finds only continuity: Transplant wings under construction, business as usual.

Profits drive hospital production. But what drives the Party? I don't pretend to have special insight into that black box other than the Marxist practice of covering up a crime against humanity by liquidating anyone who is familiar with the crime. Perhaps that explains why 500 Falun Gong are examined in a single day, or given blood tests in their homes, or why Uyghur neighborhoods are riddled with forced disappearances.

As I turn to policy, let me begin with what we can't be done.

We cannot solve this problem by pretending that prisoners of conscience have not been harvested. A Chinese doctor testified to congress on the harvesting of death-row prisoners in 2001. It caused a ripple, not a wave. We are here today, side by side, because the people in this room are concerned about prisoners of conscience.

We cannot verify self-proclaimed medical reform by arranged visits to a few Chinese transplant hospitals. In the words of Dr. Jacob Lavee, from The Transplantation Society (TTS) ethics committee and Doctors Against Forced Organ Harvesting (DAFOH):

> "As a son of a Holocaust survivor, I feel obliged to not repeat the dreadful mistake made by the International Red Cross visit to the Theresienstadt Nazi concentration camp in 1944, in which it was reported to be a pleasant recreation camp."

In short, the medical community cannot solve this problem alone. They need House Resolution 343. They need our research—and new investigations. They need to have oversight over Americans going to China for organs—and the support of the American people.

According to Lavee, not a single Israeli has gone to China for a transplant since Israel took a stand against organ tourism in 2008. Cutting off HMO funding wasn't enough; the Israeli surgeons needed to make the point that no matter how much Chinese money was invested in Israeli software, doctors have a special interest in the phrase "never again." For Taiwan, rejecting organ tourism to China was even more courageous given the Chinese military threat. But if the Taiwanese medical establishment and the political sector can join hands, we can too.

I have been told this is a Falun Gong issue. No, this is the familiar specter of human genocide—cloaked in modern scrubs. Even with a united effort, we may lose the patient. Yet let us at least enter the operating room with clean hands.

STATEMENT OF FRANCIS L. DELMONICO, M.D, PROFESSOR OF SURGERY, HARVARD MEDICAL SCHOOL

Dr. DELMONICO. Thank, Mr. Chairman, for the opportunity to make these comments.

I would like you both to know that I agree with the other individuals that are making testimony today. The use of organs from the executed prisoners is condemnable. It is a reprehensible practice.

It is a disgraceful practice because of the corruption. It is a corruption intended to acquire money and not provide care.

I want to share with you an anecdote that is illustrative and I would like to say to both of you that I have been to 70 countries around this world in the last decade to combat organ trafficking.

In a visit to Riyadh, Saudi Arabia, the physician who is sitting next to me at dinner tells me of this incident—the mother of a 14-year-old—14-year-old—who undergoes a kidney transplant in Tianjin, China and returns home to Saudi Arabia and ill within days of the transplant.

This patient undergoes a biopsy of the kidney because the kidney is not working, to discover that the kidney is scarred. It is obsolescent. It is not going to function. It never can function, and it has been at that time removed from an individual that is an executed prisoner.

This patient, Mr. Chairman, then develops a viral infection, this 14-year-old, and that infection should have been prevented by medicines that should have been administered at the time of the transplant. And the end of the story is that she dies. It cost the mother $200,000 in cash for her child to die.

That is why I am in the midst of this issue of organ trafficking as a professional not to enable that to happen not only in China but anyplace else in this world.

So it becomes a very corrupt practice by the chain from the prison to the patient ward. But I think you both have to know that it is not just from within China.

Patients from the United States and Israel and Canada and yes, I know Mr. Gutmann is talking about J. Levee, who is a good friend of mine, and I know what the Israelis have done to prevent Israelis from going to other locations in this world. But it has been there and it has been from Saudi Arabia and Canada and Japan that patients go into China.

That practice is now stopping. Over the course of this last decade I have gotten to know someone within China that you know in the media—Jiefu Huang—and I want to say to you that from my perspective he's a courageous leader because change is occurring in China.

And I know of this by Mr. Gutmann's comment. I have been to many cities now within China and been with the younger people who are doing the transplants and their future is not to use organs from the executed because the transplantation community of the world will not let them make presentations about those data and they, in their interest to propel their careers, are coming away from that practice.

They are no longer using that organ source, and the alternative of having deceased donors within the intensive care units is becoming the source of organ donors.

I know of this as well because of the risk that has been personal risk to Jiefu Huang to stay within China and make for that change to occur. I know of that personal risk as well for his mentee, his young leader that he has mentored who was under house arrest for months, that we weren't able to reach him.

He's a member of the same committee that Mr. Gutmann is talking about. Jay Levee is in that committee of the Transplantation Society. Jiefu Huang is a member of that committee. We couldn't have at him for months.

But the practice is now changing and he was released. It was also through an effort that we wrote to President Xi Jinping an open letter that was published in the medical literature to call upon China to stop the corrupt practice.

So I am with the presenters to say to you we agree completely on this being a condemnable practice. But it is my responsibility and the leadership of the international transplant community to go there and try and make change, and we are trying to do that.

And so in my visits and having patient contact, being in the wards to see what's going on, I can say to you that that experience is not with the use of executed prisoners any longer and I have some then hope and optimism that the practice will come about to stop and change.

Can I assure you that it is completely eradicated? No, I can't. But that is not my job here to make that assurance to you. My job is to say to you that the international community does not accept that practice.

The international community must work with its Chinese colleagues to change that practice and that is what has been our objective.

And to make this system of organ donation and transplantation in China consistent with the guiding principles of the World Health Organization that yours truly helped to write and develop, and with the Declaration of Istanbul.

Again, as you've mentioned, Mr. Chairman, the practice of organ trafficking is not isolated to China. You can read last week of the revelation in India and I can tell you about it in Egypt and in the Philippines and in other locations of the world.

So I would agree with Dr. Matas about his request for China to consider extraterritorial jurisdiction about the crime of organ trafficking that has now been made plain, clear as a money transaction by the Council of Europe.

We need to help the State Department to organize its TIP report—its annual report on the trafficking of human persons. We need to make certain that the organ trafficking component is made in that edition as well.

And lastly, I wish to say that if Congress wants to stop—combat organ trafficking, it can sustain a resolve not to permit organ sales in the United States.

So thank you for the opportunity to make these comments. I look forward to your questions and to elaborate further upon what has been a decade of experience in this issue.

[The prepared statement of Dr. Delmonico follows:]

HARVARD MEDICAL SCHOOL   **MASSACHUSETTS GENERAL HOSPITAL**

FRANCIS L. DELMONICO, M.D.
Professor of Surgery

Senior Surgeon
Massachusetts General Hospital
Boston Massachusetts 02114-2696
Telephone (617) 726-2825
Fax (617) 726-9039
E-mail: francis_delmonico@neob.org

June 23, 2016

Thank you for the opportunity to provide this testimony to the Subcommittee on Global Human Rights, particularly focusing upon the allegation "that China is engaged in the theft of organs on a large scale".

Please know that I agree with the other individuals who have been asked to testify that the use of organs from the executed prisoner is a condemnable and reprehensible practice, whether in China or has been proposed in Utah.

It became a disgraceful practice in China because of the corruption--- a corruption intended to acquire money but certainly not to provide care. Permit me to share an anecdote that is illustrative. I have visited more than 70 countries in this world with a goal of combating organ trafficking. In one such visit to Riyadh, Saudi Arabia, the physician sitting next to me at dinner told me of this incident: the mother of a 14-year-old girl who underwent a kidney transplant in Tianjin, China, and return home to Saudi Arabia ill. This patient underwent a biopsy of a kidney transplant to discover the kidney was obsolescent, scarred, certainly not suitable for transplantation. It had been obtained from an executed prisoner. This patient subsequently developed a viral infection that should've been prophylactically treated at the time of the transplant in China. This 14-year-old girl died within weeks of her transplant because of that derelict care, it cost the mother $200,000 for her daughter to die.

It became corrupt with everyone in the chain of the activity from the prison to the patient ward--- it became corrupt by soliciting patients from the United States from Israel from Saudi Arabia, from Egypt, from Canada from anywhere to entice desperate individuals with money.

Meanwhile, over the course of the past decade, a courageous leader in China Jiefu Huang has been the principal ally to change this outrageous practice.

Whether --as contended by others making testimony at this hearing-he may have sanctioned the practice of recovering organs from executed prisoners-- rationalizing that such prisoners should have the option of remedying at the time of death, the offense that rendered capital punishment-- there should be no setting aside the leadership of Jiefu Huang in changing China.

I know this change ---by the personal risk that he and his mentee Haibo Wang have suffered. Haibo was placed under house arrest for months because of his alliance with the international community to change this practice.

In 2006, more than 11,000 transplants were performed in China on foreign patients. This year, in 2016, we are anticipating more than 4000 deceased donors with organs recovered from such donors hospitalized in the intensive care units in China with none designated for foreign patients.

I know this from a correspondence to President Xi Jinping of China enabled by Jiefu Huang and published in the medical literature that focused upon "China's Fight against Corruption in Organ Transplantation".

Following that correspondence, the State Council of China ruled that as of January 2015 use of organs from executed prisoners would be prohibited.

I know this from multiple visits to China developing an infrastructure that will enable change.

We are underway with a different China. Is it completely resolved ? No, I cannot make that assurance But China is implementing in virtually all major cities that authorize organ transplantation-- approximately 170 transplant centers a new protocol. I can assure the members of the Subcommittee that we will continue to work diligently to achieve this goal: that the practice of organ donation and transplantation in China is consistent with Guiding Principles of the World Health Organization and the Declaration of Istanbul.

The unethical practice of organ trafficking and transplant tourism has not been isolated to China. One can readily read in the media of the recent exposure of organ sales in India—by vendors, who are destitute, with nothing but a kidney ss a commodity for them to sell.

If this Congress wants to combat organ trafficking in China and in Mexico and in the Philippines and in Egypt and in Pakistan and Vietnam--- we need the help of the State Department to collect data on organ trafficking in its annual report on trafficking in human persons (TIPS).

If this Congress wants to combat organ trafficking it can sustain a resolve not to permit organs for sale in the United States.

I look forward to questions from the committee and again I wish to convey my appreciation for the opportunity to make these comments.

Sincerely yours,

Francis L. Delmonico, M.D.

World Health Organization
Advisory for Human Transplantation

Mr. ROHRABACHER. Thank you, sir.

And Dr. Lee.

STATEMENT OF CHARLES LEE, M.D., DIRECTOR OF PUBLIC AWARENESS, WORLD ORGANIZATION TO INVESTIGATE THE PERSECUTION OF FALUN GONG

Dr. LEE. Thank you, Chairman Smith and Rohrabacher, members of the committees and the staff members. My testimony has four sections.

Section one is WOIPFG and its investigations into organ harvesting. World Organization to Investigate and Persecution of Falun Gong was established on January 20th, 2003.

Up to May 2016 we have published 331 investigative reports and have compiled a list of more than 76,000 individual perpetrators. We have systematically investigated on the crimes on the forced organ harvesting over the last 10 years and we have published 43 reports.

In June 2015, we published a comprehensive report over here in which we laid out 1,628 pieces of evidence proving that more than 865 hospitals and more than 9,500 surgeons in China who have been involved in these huge number of transplant operations.

We have conducted more than 10,000 telephone interviews with Chinese Government officials and the surgeons, procured 60 recording testimonies from high-ranking government officials including five CCP Politburo standing committee members.

These testimonies reveal that the majority of the extracted organs were from leading Falun Gong practitioners and that the order came from the CCP's highest level.

Since then, we have published another nine additional reports confirming that the organ harvesting on Falun Gong practitioners is still happening and in some places might be accelerating.

We have another report over here. We would like to submit these two reports to the Congress for the record. So far we have—actually, my focus today will be the academic papers published by the doctors inside of China, mostly from year 2000 through 2012.

So far, we have collected more than 3,000 academic papers. Three hundred of them have descriptions on donors. We have found evidence proving the existence of the large organ living donor pool, strengthening the previous conclusion of harvesting organs from living persons by the CCP.

They are the written testimonies in the public domain provided by those doctors who have been involved in this heinous crime.

Section two—medical papers and publications indicate that a huge living donor pool exists. Number one, very short waiting time; number two, in April 2006, one hospital in Hunan offered 20 livers and kidneys for free to lure more business. They have access to a very large donor pool.

Number three, the abundance of the donors have even made the Chinese medicine hospitals—forensic hospitals, psychiatric hospitals, to conduct organ transplant operations.

Number four—a large number of emergency transplant operations. China's Liver Transplant Registration Project was started in early 2005. More than 8,000 cases have been collected up to December 2006. Among 4,300 cases with available data for a timing manner, 1,150 cases were of emergency operations which was as high as 27 percent.

The shortest time to start the operation was 4 hours after the patient was admitted. The same database provides that only 2 percent of the donors were living donors. All the others were dead.

By contrast, only 6½ percent of liver transplants performed at a leading transplant center in Canada from 1994 to 2008 was for acute liver failure, which needs emergency transplant in 48 to 72 hours.

Canada has a matching system supposed to be much more efficient than anything legitimate for matching up in China. A more plausible explanation is that it is the donors wait for the recipients in China.

Number five, abundance of donors provide to multiple stand-by donors for transplantation surgeons. One typical case was Huang Jiefu—Huang Jiefu's liver transplant operation in Xinjiang on September 28th, 2005. The first donor's liver was discarded after Huang opened the abdominal cavity of a cancer patient and he discovered that it happened to meet to the criteria for a autologous liver transplant.

He then closed it and contacted Guangzhou City and Chongqing City requesting a spare liver in case the autologous transplant failed.

Matching livers were found in both cities in several hours and arrived in Xinjiang almost at the same time at 6:30 p.m. on September 29th. Another—also another spare liver was found in Xinjiang. The operation lasted from 7 o'clock p.m. on September 29th to 10 o'clock a.m. next day.

After 24 hours of observation, Huang announced the spare livers were no longer needed. The acceptable cold ischemic time for liver was less than 15 hours even in China. Therefore, one can safely say that the two spare livers brought from Chongqing and Guangzhou City could only be two intact living persons.

Otherwise, the extraction, the flight, the operation and the observation time would be at least 50 hours. The spare livers would have no value.

Section three—medical papers indicate that large scale kill on demand organ transplant system. Number one, abnormal descriptions on the donors.

One hundred three papers have information about the donors. The total number mentioned was 8,710. Eighty papers had the ages, from 20 to 40 years old with average in the 20s, while in the U.S. average age of deceased donors in 2006 was a little over 40.

The vast majority of the descriptions regarding the health condition of the donors are perfectly healthy. There is no history of contagious disease, cardiovascular disease, cancer or drug abuse, et cetera.

One might wonder why these young and perfectly healthy people would donate their organs and die. Number two, brain death in China—a simplified definition of brain death is the death of all central neurological tissue, resulting in the loss of cerebral functions.

Strict procedures and long-term observing should be implemented before announcing the brain death. In the U.S., there were about 6,700 living donors and 8,000 deceased donors in 2006. The three major causes of deaths were cerebral vascular stroke, head trauma and anoxia, anoxia brain deaths.

B, in China there is no legal definition or procedure to follow to announce a person is brain dead. One article on Tengxun net in 2014 cited Huang Jiefu, stating that 90 percent of the doctors in China don't know the criteria for brain deaths.

It was still not a good time for China to enact a brain death law. One hundred thirty-seven papers described the causes of the deaths in over 5,000 donors. Fifty-nine percent were brain deaths. Further analysis and review that the vast majority of these brain deaths were actually living people.

C, China's leading expert on brain death, Chen Zhonghua from Tongji Medical College, has been exploring using internationally accepted brain death criteria in organ transplantations.

An article by his group in Journal of Organ Transplant in July 2010 stating that 60 cases of organ extractions were conducted from brain death donors in China since 2001. That's 10 years period of time.

In July 2006, they conducted the first ever heart transplantation using a brain death donor in the country. Chen Zhonghua's numbers clearly indicated that to the vast majority of these cases of extractions are not from truly brain death donors.

Because it is not a legal practice at all in China to announce a patient is brain dead and that there is no formal training or certifications for the doctors, they should be still alive when the organs were taken.

D, we found five papers with 22 cases describing the procedure of tracheal intubination after the brain deaths. This makes no medical sense. The diagnosis of brain death needs hours of observation and the testings.

Tracheal intubation should be—and the tracheal intubation should be done in the process or before that in order to save the life of the patient.

These doctors have confirmed that they didn't—they did not understand the criteria for brain deaths nor did they care if the donors were brain dead. The donors were actually living people.

E, the other three major causes of death in the papers—cadaver, sudden death and no heart beating—did not give any information on how these donors died either.

Number three, extremely short ischemic time. Warm ischemic time here refers to the amount of time that an organ remains warm after its blood supply has been stopped or reduced.

Eighty-nine papers had close to 7,000 cases on the warm ischemic time from donors with brain death, cadaver or sudden death. Most of them is under 10 minutes. Some mentioned the cause of the deaths.

Six hundred eighty-eight cases were brain dead—brain death. One had 117 cases of fresh cadavers with heart beats just stopped. With brain death not practicable and almost no explainable legitimate cause of death, then why almost all organ documents have such short one ischemic time? The most plausible explanation is that these donors have been arranged to die when the organ procurements need to happen. This is mass murder.

Section four—in six papers 42 doctors admittedly have killed at least 677 living people for their organs. Number one, general transplants, May 2011, Yang Shou-guo, et cetera, from a transplantation center in Shanghai described 298 cases of heart transplantation in 11 years from May 2000.

On donor descriptions it reads 291 hearts were from cadavers. Seven hearts were from brain dead donors 18 to 45 years old, average 27. All donors had no obvious history of cardiovascular disease or other major organ diseases.

Among these 298 cases, after year 2007, 60 hearts were extracted when the donors had ventricle fibrillation, or after the heart stopped beating and that the rest were extracted while the hearts were still beating.

The authors admitted here that at least 231 healthy young people while not brain dead and that their hearts were still beating were killed for their hearts.

Number two—Chinese general practice December 2007, Li Yao-feng, et cetera, talked about 103 liver transplantations beginning in 2004 in the center. It reads, the donors of both groups of recipients were healthy young people.

One of them was brain dead. All others were same blood type, cadaveric livers. All ischemic times were between 0 and 5 minutes.

The conclusion should be easy to draw. At least 102 young people had been killed for their organs.

Number three—Chinese Journal Hepatobiliary——

Mr. SMITH. Dr. Lee——

(Off mic comments)

Dr. LEE. Okay. That's fine. I have, you know, three more but these are the published academic papers in which those doctors actually, you know, admit they have killed people while they are alive.

The accounts show that the practice of forced organ harvest is real and is done on a very large scale. I am going to submit these six papers to the Congress for the record and we are going to take some time to translate all of them. But these are real published papers.

Thank you very much. Actually, we have——

Mr. ROHRABACHER. Without objection, they will be put into the record.

Dr. LEE. All right. Thank you.

[The prepared statement of Dr. Lee follows:]

ORGAN HARVESTING: AN EXAMINATION OF A BRUTAL PRACTICE

COMMITTEE ON FOREIGN AFFAIRS HEARING

Subcommittee on Africa, Global Health, Global Human Rights,
and International Organizations
Christopher Smith (R-NJ), Chairman
&
Subcommittee on Europe, Eurasia, and Emerging Threats
Dana Rohrabacher (R-CA), Chairman

2:00 PM Thursday June 23, 2016
Room 2200, Rayburn House Office Building

**Medical Papers and Official Publications from China
Show Mass Murder for Organ Transplants**

Charles Lee, M.D., Director of Public Awareness,

World Organization to Investigate the Persecution of Falun Gong (WOIPFG)

Thank you, Chairman Chris Smith and Chairman Dana Rohrabacher, committee members and staff, for giving me the chance to testify here. I would also like to thank Mr. David Matas, Mr. David Kilgour, and Mr. Ethan Gutmann for standing together with us to expose these heinous crimes that have never taken place before in human history.

1. WOIPFG and Its Investigations into Organ Harvesting

WOIPFG was established on January 20, 2003, with the mission to investigate the criminal actions of all institutions, organizations, and individuals involved in the persecution of Falun Gong; to bring such investigations, no matter how long they take, no matter how far and deep we have to search, to full closure; to protect the fundamental principles of humanity; and to restore and uphold justice in society. As of May 10, 2016, we have published 331 investigative reports on the persecution of Falun Gong, totaling 5.8 million words. We have compiled a list of 76,132 individual perpetrators, and 35,551 responsible institutions.

The explosion of the organ transplant industry in China since the persecution on Falun Gong began has resulted in many investigations into forced organ harvesting from prisoners of conscience, especially from practitioners of Falun Gong.

WOIPFG has been systematically investigating forced organ harvesting since this crime was brought to light on March 9, 2006.

Over the past ten years, WOIPFG has published 43 reports on forced organ harvesting. We published a comprehensive report in June, 2015 (http://www.zhuichaguoji.org/node/48095 Chinese, http://www.upholdjustice.org/node/338 English, 3rd version), in which we laid out 1,628 pieces of evidence from hospital websites and medical journals, among others, showing that over 865 hospitals and over 9,500 surgeons in China have been involved in a huge number of transplant operations. We have conducted more than ten thousands of telephone interviews with Chinese government officials, as well as surgeons in the hospitals, and have procured 60 secretly recorded telephone calls from five current or former CCP Politburo Standing Committee members, one vice-chairman of the Central Military Commission (CMC), one CCP Politburo member, one CMC member and former defense minister, one department head of the People's Liberation Army General Logistics Department's Health Division, an armed guard who witnessed live organ harvesting, as well as several senior officials from the Political and Legislative Affairs Committee, Red Cross Donation Office, Surgeons from more than 30 hospitals. These recordings collectively indicate that the majority of the extracted organs came from the bodies of living Falun Gong practitioners, and that the order to harvest organs from Falun Gong practitioners came from the CCP's highest levels.

Since then, WOIPFG has published 9 additional reports providing evidence that organ harvesting of Falun Gong practitioners is still happening in China, and may in some places even be accelerating—all while China has yet to implement reform of its practices, and while the volunteer-based donation system it says it's building relies on promises by officials who have a track record of lying (http://www.upholdjustice.org/node/330).

My focus today will be on medical papers published by doctors inside China, mostly from the year 2000 to 2012.

So far, WOIPFG has collected more than 3,000 academic papers on organ transplants in China and has analyzed over 300 of them, with descriptions of donors from over 200 hospitals in 31 provinces and municipalities in China. Nearly all of them were written after 1999, especially between the years of 2000 and 2008. By analyzing the descriptions of the gender, age, health condition and cause of death of the "donors," the procedure of organ removal, the data on the warm and cold ischemia time (that is, respectively, the time from the cessation of circulation until the perfusion of the organ with cold preservative chemicals; and the time from when the organ is perfused until it is transplanted into the recipient) and the rapidity of organ matching, we are able to point to the clear existence of a large organ "donor" bank consisting of *living* persons. This new set of evidence also strengthens the previous conclusion that the Chinese regime is harvesting organs from living people, and that very large numbers of captive and healthy Falun Gong practitioners have been kept as living "donors." It also corresponds with written testimonies in the public domain provided by individuals who we believe to be whistleblower doctors who have been involved in this unprecedented crime.

2. Medical Papers and Publications Inside China Indicate That a Huge Living Donor Pool Exists

1) Very short waiting times have been cited many times before as one of the pieces of evidence of the donor pool.

2) A large number of emergency transplant operations. The China Liver Transplant Registration (CLTR) project was started in February, 2005. 8,486 cases have been collected as of December, 2006 from 29 transplant centers. Among 4,331 cases with available data for timing manner, *1,150 cases were emergency operations, which was as high as 26.6%.* **The fastest liver transplant operation was started only 4 hours after the patient was admitted.** The very same database provides that *97.7% of the liver donors were cadavers, living (relatives) donors accounted for only 2%.*

By contrast, out of the 919 liver transplants performed at Multi-Organ Transplant Programme, London Health Sciences Centre in Canada from 1994 to 2008, 60 were performed on patients for acute liver failure (ALF), which was only 6.5%. Emergency liver transplant is needed for those who have ALF and transplantation should be performed in 48-72 hours. Canada has a waiting list/donor registration system; those with ALF are assigned with the highest priorities, the system is supposed to be much more efficient than the one in China, where there's no waiting list system or donation system available for matching up.

Given that China had no effective national matching system during this period, it seems the only reasonable explanation for these rapid matching times is the **donors wait for recipients in China.**

3) An abundance of donors provides multiple standby donors for transplantation surgeons. One typical case was Huang Jiefu's liver transplant operation in Xinjiang in September, 2005. Huang was then the vice minister of the Ministry of Health. The 1st donor's liver was discarded due to the discovery that the patient was suitable for autologous liver transplant. Then he called for another three "standby livers" from three different places: Chongqing, Guangzhou and Xinjiang.

According to reports on the website "China Nurse" and two other websites, on the afternoon of September 28, 2005, while attending the 50th anniversary celebration of the Chinese Communist Party's occupation of Xinjiang, Huang Jiefu demonstrated a transplant operation at the First Affiliated Hospital of Xinjiang Medical University. After Huang opened the abdominal cavity of a cancer patient, he discovered that the patient's liver happened to meet the criteria for an autologous liver transplant, which he had dreamed about performing. . He then closed the abdominal opening, and immediately contacted one hospital in Guangzhou City and one liver medical center in Chongqing City, requesting them to provide a spare liver each, in case the autologous liver transplant failed. Matching livers were quickly found in both cities, and the matching livers arrived in Xinjiang almost at the same time, at 6:30 p.m. on September 29.

Huang's operation lasted from 7 p.m. on September 29 to 10 a.m. on September 30. After 24 hours of observation, Huang announced that the operation was successful; therefore, the spare livers were no longer needed.

The acceptable cold ischemic time (that is, the time from when an organ is cooled and perfused with chemicals as it is removed from the donor, until it is transplanted) for a liver is 6-10 hours. In China it is sometimes longer, but should still be within 15 hours. *Therefore, one can safely say that the "two spare livers" brought from Chongqing and Guangzhou could only be two intact living persons,* otherwise, the extraction time, flight time, Huang's operation time and observation time would be at least 50 hours, the livers would have no value. *Yet they were called spare livers.*

4) An abundance of donors results in hospitals promoting organs in the market and offering *"free" transplant operations.* On April 28, 2006, Hunan People's Hospital offered 20 livers and kidneys for free to the public in order to attract more business. There have been many promotions like this. WOIPFG has complete archives of this material and we are happy to share our findings with researchers and government.

5) The abundance of donors has even made *Chinese medicine hospitals, forensic hospitals, psychiatric hospitals to conduct organ transplant operations.*

3. Medical Papers From China Indicate a Large-Scale "Kill on Demand" Organ Transplant System

1) Abnormal descriptions of donors

Among 300 research papers, 103 papers have information about the donors, such as gender, age, cause of death, blood type, and various other test results.

The total number of donors referred to in the 103 research papers is 8,710.

Among the 5,266 donors with information on gender, 97% were male. 80 papers had the age of the donors, which was 20 to 40-years-old. Many papers indicate an average age in the twenties, while in the U.S., the average age of deceased donors in 2006 was a little over 40-years-old.

With the papers we have examined, the vast majority of the descriptions regarding the health condition of the "donors" are *perfectly healthy;* no contagious diseases, sexually transmitted diseases, cardiovascular diseases, cancer or any drug abuse history.

One is forced to wonder: Is this the typical health profile of a criminal? Might there not be healthy and young innocent people among those being killed for their organs, and written up in these studies?

2) Brain death in China

a) A simplified definition of brain death is the death of all of central neurological tissue resulting in the loss of cerebral function, and the demonstration of any cerebral function precludes the diagnosis. Since it is a matter of life and death, strict procedures of examining and long-term observations of the patient are complied before announcing the patient is brain-dead, and the doctors need to be authorized to do it.

In the U.S., there were 8,024 deceased donors and 6,732 living donors in 2006. Regarding the cause of death among the deceased organ donors, 38% died from head trauma, 17% was anoxia brain death, and about 43% was cerebro-vascular stroke.

b) Brain death in China is still a concept that has been explored and experimented on. There is no legal definition or procedure to follow. One article on Tengxun Net on 8/22/2014 cited Huang Jiefu, the official spokesperson for China's organ transplantation industry for many years, stating that 90% of the doctors in China don't know the criteria for brain death. It was still not a good time for China to enact a brain death law.

Among the 137 papers collected by WOIPFG regarding the causes of death of the 5,093 donors, 3,007 (59%) of them are classified as "brain dead." The classification is used to highlight that the quality of the organs are good, since the heartbeat continued until the moment before the organs were removed. Further analysis of the papers indicates that the vast majority of these supposed brain dead donors were almost certainly actually living people. The other three major causes of death in these papers were "cadaver," "sudden death" and "non-heart beating" donors.

c) The leading expert on brain death in China, Chen Zhonghua from Tongji Medical College in Wuhan, has explored using the internationally accepted brain death criteria in organ transplantation. His study is directly supported by the Chinese Ministries of Health and Education. An article published by his group in the Journal of Organ Transplant (Chinese version) in July 2010 stated that 60 cases of organ extraction were conducted from brain-dead donors in China since 2001. On July 1, 2006, they conducted the first ever heart transplantation using a brain dead donor in China.

d) The comparison between Chen's number with the number on other papers regarding the brain dead donor numbers, it is clear that the vast majority of *these cases of extraction are not from truly brain dead donors* , because it is not a legal practice at all in China to announce a patient brain dead and there is no formal training and certifications from doctors. If they were surgically treated as brain dead, yet were not truly brain dead, then they could only have been alive when their organs were extracted. *The other three major causes of death (cadaver, sudden death, no heart beating) did not give any information on how these donors died, either.*

e) We found 5 papers with 22 cases describing tracheal intubation after supposed brain death. This makes no medical sense. The diagnosis of brain death is time consuming, requiring sometimes hours of observation and repeated testing. Tracheal intubation should be done in the diagnosis process or before that, in order to save the life of the patient. One of the key tests for brain death is to turn off the ventilator – after intubation – and see whether the patient breaths by him or herself. If that does not happen, the patient may be declared brain dead. These doctors have confirmed that (1) **they didn't understand the criteria for brain death, (2) they didn't care if the donors were brain dead, (3) and therefore, the only other possibility is that the donors were actually living people,** and that the tracheal intubation and anesthesia referred to in the papers were employed to ensure organs in their best condition.

3) Extremely short warm ischemic times

Warm ischemic time refers to the amount of time that an organ remains warm after its blood supply has been stopped or reduced. At this point it is quickly perfused with preservative chemical and cooled, then procured and placed in a bag with preservative solution.

In the event of brain dead organ recovery, the warm ischemic time is very minimal, because the heart stops only moments before the organs are cooled. For a DCD (donation after cardiac death) organ recovery, warm ischemic time includes the amount of time that the organ is not being properly perfused prior to death, the 5 minute waiting period following death, and the time that it takes for cannulation to occur and to get the flushes and icing started.

With over 300 papers we have examined, 89 papers with 6,759 cases specifically talking about the warm ischemic time from the so-called "brain death", cadaver or sudden death donors, most of the warm ischemia time is under 10 minutes, some are even zero minutes. Some of the 89 papers described the cause of the death, 688 cases were brain death, one paper mentioned 117 cases were "fresh cadavers whose heart beat just stopped."

With "brain death" not practicable, and almost no explainable, legitimate cause of death, then why did almost all organ procurements have such short warm ischemia times, with many of them even being under a minute? The most plausible explanation is that most of these donors have been arranged to die when the organ procurement needs to happen. We know that these were not voluntary donors, and we know that the operation was scheduled in advance, because the recipient was already ready for the organ (given the short cold ischemic times.) This required blood-matching. Thus, **the donors must have been killed for the purpose of having their organs removed.**

This is mass murder.

4. In 6 Papers, 42 Doctors Admit

They Have Killed at Least 677 Living People for the organs

1) For the first paper, for the Congressional record, I would like to read the Chinese first

中华移植杂志(电子版)2011年5月第5卷第2期, 第10-14页　扬守国等 复旦大学器官移植中心 "298例原位心脏移植受者远期疗效分析"

第10页. 2000年5月至2011年4月,

第11页. . 1.2 供者与共资料与供心保存

尸体供心291例，临床脑死亡7例。年龄18～45岁，平均（26.8±4.5）岁。其中男性283例，女性15例。均无明确心血管疾病或其他重大脏器疾病史。供心获取方法与以前的报道相同。在298例中，自2007年后有60例供心在心室颤动或心搏停止状态下获取，其余在心脏仍搏动时获取。

"Long-term results of 298 cases of orthotropic heart transplantations: a single center experience"

By Yang Shou-guo etc (transplantation center of Fudan University) Chinese J Transplant May 2011, Vol 5 No 2. Pages 10-14 (http://www.zhuichaguoji.org/en/images/medicalarticles/79.pdf)

page 10 May 2000 to April 2011,

page 11 Section 1.2 Donors' information and preservation of donors' hearts:

291 hearts were from cadavers, 7 hearts were from brain-dead donors. They were 18 to 45-years-old. Average age is 26.8(±4.5). 283 male and 15 female. All "donors" had no obvious history of cardiovascular diseases or other major organ diseases. The procuring methods of the hearts were the same as previously reported. Among these 298 cases, after 2007, 60 hearts were extracted when the donors had ventricular fibrillation or after the heart stopped beating, and the rest were extracted while the heart was still beating.

The authors indicate here that **at least 231 healthy young people**, while not brain dead and with their heart still beating, were put in hospital beds and **killed for their hearts**.

2) "Different Modes Operandi Analysis of Liver Function in Liver Transplantation Perioperation" by Li Yao-feng, etc. Chinese General Practice Dec 2007, Vol 10 No 23.

103 liver transplants between 2004 and 2007. Operation methods: the donors for both groups of recipients were healthy young people, one of them was brain-dead... all others were the same blood type cadaveric livers, all warm ischemia times were between zero and 5 minutes.

The conclusion should be easy to draw with these elements: all healthy and young "donors", warm ischemia times of 0-5 minutes, all were cadaveric except for one person who was brain-dead... **at lest 102 young people should have been killed for their organs**.

3) "Clinical study on techniques for cadaveric total evisceration" by Sun Xuyang etc from PLA 303 Hospital in Nanning City, Guangxi Province, Chinese Journal of Hepatobiliary Surgery May 2006, Vol 12. No 5. (http://www.zhuichaguoji.org/cn/images/medicalarticles/168.pdf)

The authors describe 72 cases of multi-organ abdominal extractions between June, 2003 and June, 2005. All donors were cadaveric, 62 male cases, 10 female cases, aged 18-41, average 27-years-old. ... 2 hours before the operation, 200 mg of heparin was injected intramuscularly. On the next page they described the results, warm ischemia time was (2.2 ± 0.6) minutes, the time to establish the low temperature perfusion system was (1.7± 0.4) minutes.

If you put these three events together: 1) heparin (a blood thinner, used to prevent clotting) injection two hours before the operations; 2) the operations; and 3) procurements of the organs with warm ischemia time at 2.2 minutes, it is very clear that **all 72 donors were arranged to be killed for their organs**. And they were all young.

4) The same Journal published an article in February, 2007, Vol 13, No 2 by Shen Zhongyang from Tianjin First Central Hospital. They described the extraction of livers from **200 cadaveric donors** from September, 2003 to November, 2005. They described the donors as non-heart beating cadavers. But they also injected heparin 2-3 hours before the operation and the warm ischemia time was less than 8 minutes. Shen Zhongyang has been listed as one of the worst doctors in China by WOIPFG. Chinese official sources say that he has performed or directly overseen nearly 10,000 liver transplantations as of December, 2014.

5) "Clinical Application of Combined Liver-Kidney Procuring Techniques on Non Heart Beating Donors" by Yuan Xiaopeng etc at Dept of Organ Transplant, Taiping Hospital in Dongwuan City, Guangdong Province, Hainan J of Medicine, 2006, Vol 17, No 2. (http://www.zhuichaguoji.org/cn/images/medicalarticles/20101.pdf, http://www.zhuichaguoji.org/cn/images/medicalarticles/20102.pdf)

Data on Donors: Donors were all non-heart beating donors, aged at 20-30 years old, liver function test all normal; HBsAg, HBeAg, HBeAb, HCV -Ab, HEV-Ab, HIV-Ab HPR, TPPA were all negative. **1hr before cutting the organs, the donors were injected 10 mg Phentolamine intramuscularly, 400 mg Heparin intravenously.**

It is obvious that one hour before the procuring the organs, the donors were all alive.

6) "Two cases of combined heart lung transplantation, CHLT, the extraction and the preservation of donors' heart and lung" by Jian Wu at Yanan Hospital of Kunming City, *Yunnan Journal of Medicine and Pharmaceutics* 2008 Volume 29 Issue 5

Operational procedures: After the donors entered the operation room, they were treated with routine anesthesia and endotracheal intubation, they were treated with intravenous injection of 1g of Methylprednisolone Sodium Succinate (Sou-Medrol), and heparin (3mg/kg). *After the anesthesia took effect,* routine disinfection was conducted and the cloth was laid on, the cut was taken right in the middle.

With the description of the usage of anesthesia and heparin, it is clear **that the donors were alive when they entered the operation room**. Then their lungs and hearts were harvested together.

All these are written testimonies from doctors in China who have been involved in these activities, which appear to collectively add up to mass murder. Their accounts show that the practice of forced organ harvesting is real and done on a very large scale.

We appeal to the U.S. Government to:

*   Commission an independent investigation into this crime against humanity;

*   Openly condemn the communist regime's practice of forced organ harvesting and urge it to end immediately;

*   We also appeal to the State Department to share any materials it has gained about these activities, and to produce a detailed report based on its own research as well as the findings here today;

*   Enact a law to prevent Americans from going to China for organ tourism;

*   To enact laws to deny visas to perpetrators of forced organ harvesting, and to subject them to legal proceedings if they are already in the United States.

Thank you very much.

Mr. ROHRABACHER. You know, some of us we had a rather tumultuous night last night and there was—so we didn't get much sleep so I apologize for being a little groggy here.

Let's go into some questions and answers. Now, I am going to get an understanding of what we are talking about here, the basis, and Dr. Delmonico, you might tell me how long does it—you have when someone dies, whether they are killed or whether they just died, how long do you—do you have before that organ is no longer transmittable to another person?

Dr. DELMONICO. Depends on the organ. Depends on the organ, Mr. Chairman. So the heart is very sensitive. Once it arrests, it becomes complicated for you to be able to transplant it.

The kidneys can last an hour without circulation and still be recovered and transplanted.

Mr. ROHRABACHER. So it is 1 hour for a kidney?

Dr. DELMONICO. For kidneys. But that is why I am saying to you it depends on the organ. So the heart is very sensitive. Once it arrests and has no circulation it becomes complicated to make a successful transplant. But there is research that is being done now to do them.

But in terms of China and what has been practiced, once the heart arrests it becomes very difficult to transplant it—unpredictable. The lungs can last for a couple of hours because there is oxygen retained within the lung even after circulation subsides. The liver can be no more than about 30 minutes without sufficient circulation and it has to be transplanted, otherwise it won't function.

So there is a sensitivity of each organ to ischemia, or an absence of circulation, that makes it different from one organ to another.

Mr. ROHRABACHER. How about the——

Dr. DELMONICO. Yes, sir.

Mr. ROHRABACHER [continuing]. The cornea in your eyes?

Dr. DELMONICO. The corneas can be—that is a tissue and that is a different matter. It doesn't require circulation. It can be recovered many hours after the individual has died.

Mr. ROHRABACHER. And how long will it last before it has to be transplanted?

Dr. DELMONICO. They can be preserved and transplanted days or months later—the cornea.

Mr. ROHRABACHER. And but the other organs you were talking about have to be transplanted in a matter of hours.

Dr. DELMONICO. They have to be transplanted in some proximity. Now, we are—we are in a research way these days of preserving organs that could last for a couple of days and done by placing these organs on a machine that can give the organs blood and oxygen or cold perfusate and it enables them to last for hours and then a couple of days.

Mr. ROHRABACHER. Does Dr. Delmonico's analysis—do you have any comment on it from the rest of the panel? Is that accurate?

Mr. MATAS. In terms of the times, I mean, that is scientific evidence.

Dr. DELMONICO. This has been a practice for 40 years.

Mr. MATAS. Yes. But my comment on it is that it shows that, well, except for corneas there has to be a pretty quick turnaround between the death of a source and the transplantation. We can't even have several hours. We're looking at minutes—60 minutes, maybe 2 hours in the case of one type of organ.

So and what we see in China is sometimes transplantation is scheduled on demand of the patient, short waiting times, so that—we do not have patients waiting for organs very often but rather organs waiting for patients, which means, especially in the case of vital organs, that people are being killed for their organs.

Mr. ROHRABACHER. Okay. So the—what we should be looking at then is not necessarily organs that are put into the icebox and flown somewhere but instead should be looking to people who are being recruited throughout the Western world and other countries but places where people have money who are recruited to go to China and perhaps elsewhere with other——

Dr. DELMONICO. Without question.

Mr. ROHRABACHER. Okay. So that should be a major focus as to people who are in a state of need because their own organs are being—you know, going to hell and they're giving out, and we need to be able to make sure that when they are offered here, this is your—here, how we can save you is that we are not saving them by condemning a prisoner who might be in jail for saying something bad about the Communist Party of China.

Mr. MATAS. Yes. I think all of us would agree with that statement completely.

Mr. ROHRABACHER. Let me just note, I am happy to hear this. I have been worried about this because there are transplant centers in Orange County, California and I have been very concerned that there might be some kind of organs being brought in from China. Now, is that a possibility that we——

Dr. DELMONICO. No, that is not—I should say to you, if I may——

Mr. ROHRABACHER. Sure.

Dr. DELMONICO. I had the opportunity to oversee the practice of organ donation and transplantation in this country as the president of UNOS, the United Network for Organ Sharing, that runs the practice of transplantation in the country.

Every transplant that is performed in the United States must be reported to the network—to the government, to the Department of Human Health—of Health Human Services.

So I can make some assurance to you from the system that is in the United States every transplant must be reported and there would be no opportunity of bringing organs in from China to California for a successful transplantation. Were that to be known, the centers in Orange County would be closed down that night.

Mr. ROHRABACHER. Let me—again, I am not an expert on this and what about the organ of the skin? Can skin be sent and transported?

Dr. DELMONICO. That is a tissue. So, you know, an organ is a vital structure that has blood supply, et cetera, right. But there are vital organs that require circulation for their maintenance and viability.

Mr. ROHRABACHER. Right.

Dr. DELMONICO. There are tissues such as skin and bone and cornea, valves, that do not need continuous circulation for their viability. So they can be preserved for an extended period of time or they can be processed.

Mr. ROHRABACHER. So skin is not considered an organ. For some reason back in high——

Mr. MATAS. It is a tissue, yes.

Mr. ROHRABACHER [continuing]. Back in my days when I got a D——

Dr. DELMONICO. It is under the—it is under the——

Mr. ROHRABACHER [continuing]. In health in high school, I think.

Dr. DELMONICO. Mr. Chairman, that is fine. We don't know about legislation. I will just say to you it is categorized as a tissue.

Mr. ROHRABACHER. Okay. And so whether you're saying whether it is a tissue or an organ, is there—are there cases—do we have cases where skin is being removed and being sold on a market by the Chinese Government?

Mr. MATAS. Yes. Well, that is what the plastination is. We see these body exhibits and there is some skin involved in them as well as vital organs. But, I mean, whole bodies are plastinated coming from China.

And in our update we talk about this plastination as similar fact evidence. Many of these plastinated bodies, from our conclusions, come from Falun Gong practitioners. But it is—the plastination occurs within China and the skin grafts and whatever, they occur within China.

The exportation of particular organs we don't—I mean, we have heard rumours about it. We haven't seen any evidence of it.

I wanted to pick up on what the——

Mr. ROHRABACHER. Before we go on, okay. So we haven't seen any evidence of particular organs because they—it does require time and care and it is quick. But have we seen evidence of skin transplants coming from China, the skin being transplanted and the corneas and other——

Mr. GUTMANN. I don't know. I mean, the BBC——

Mr. ROHRABACHER [continuing]. And other—these other tissue type things?

Mr. GUTMANN. The BBC comes out with a story of a collagen-based product—you know, various makeup products that use tissue from executed prisoners. They come out with that story every 3 years. It is kind of regular.

Mr. MATAS. Yes, what I wanted to say though is Dr. Delmonico had mentioned that there is compulsory reporting of all transplants within China—within the U.S.—within the U.S.

Mr. ROHRABACHER. Yes, that is—the fact is is that people go to China——

Mr. MATAS. And that is right.

Mr. ROHRABACHER [continuing]. Specifically and they are—and we have all the evidence in the world of people going there, actually perhaps as part of an organized business venture by someone who said, hey, we can get you organs and come on our—on this tour and end up at this hospital and then you have got your organ and even—and they do not know—even they have no idea——

Mr. MATAS. That is right.

Mr. ROHRABACHER [continuing]. That their—that this is coming from an involuntary donor.

Mr. MATAS. And that is not—there is no compulsory reporting for that. Once you leave and come back there is no compulsory reporting.

Mr. ROHRABACHER. Well, maybe one thing that could be done that could have an impact is that people are coming back, Chris, from China who have had some kind of organ transplant operations have to in some way show that they were in some way confident that this was not—be coming to them from an involuntary contributor.

Mr. MATAS. Well, even just at the very start at least they should be required to report—doctors and the hospitals should be required to report that this travel occurred and then there could be some investigation afterwards.

Mr. ROHRABACHER. Yes. Is there any reason why we shouldn't do that?

Dr. DELMONICO. No, no. This is fine. I am very in agreement on this one. If a patient goes to a foreign destination for a transplant and they are coming back into the United States, that is going to require sophisticated care.

Immunosuppression—the gamut of medications that have to be applied to make that organ transplant successful is sophisticated. So they are going to come home to a physician at one of our transplant centers that knows how to take care of those patients.

So our people in the United States will know if they have gone to China or to India or to Pakistan or to any location that now is doing foreign patients for money. Okay. Could even be Mexico.

Mr. ROHRABACHER. Okay. Well, this is—I will yield to Mr. Smith now and we will have a second round of questions.

Mr. SMITH. Thank you, Mr. Chairman, and thank you all for your testimonies. Very, very helpful to the subcommittees.

Just a couple of opening questions. First, to Dr. Delmonico. You mentioned Huang Jiefu and we know that he's the former Deputy Health Minister and chairman of the Human Organ Donation and Transplant Committee, among other things, and my question is—and before I get to it, I have worked human rights issues in China for 36 years, from my very first election in 1980 during the Ronald Reagan years.

Obviously Tiananmen Square was a game-changer and then, sadly, it was a major reversal for democracy and universally recognized human rights. The students were repressed.

But throughout it all, beginning of 1982, 1983 I began raising the issue of forced abortion and forced sterilization in China only to be met with aggressive denials by the Chinese Government, by the UNFPA, by many pro-abortion activists in the United States and in Europe. And in 1985, in this room, we had a hearing.

I wasn't the chairman at the time. The Democrats ran the House. And we had Foreign Service Officers telling us that it is over—it is finished, gone, and I put exclamation points on that because it was largely a 1983 high-tide experience, as they called it, and then Michael Weisskopf of the Washington Post did a three-part expose, Page 1—he was the bureau chief for the Washington Post—who absolutely blew the lid off the apologists who were out there saying there is nothing to worry about here, there is no forced abortion and no forced sterilization.

I travelled to China many times. I met with Peng Peiyun, the woman who ran the program—a face to face meeting with State Department personnel sitting there and she said these are all lies. There is no coercion whatsoever in the People's Republic of China, despite the evidence that is absolutely overwhelming and verified by all the major human rights organizations.

After Tiananmen Square I went to a gulag—a Laogai called Beijing Prison Number 1 and the Chinese Government told me that there were no political prisoners, as they have said throughout every meeting I have ever had with them.

I saw them. There were 40 of them there and the warden said 40 of these people were on the Square and they wouldn't let us talk to them.

So when Chi Haotian, the operational commander, came to the United States got a 19-gun salute by President Bill Clinton, which I thought was an abomination—here is a man who sent in the killers that crushed the dissent at Tiananmen Square

He went to the Army War College and said no one died at Tiananmen Square. In 2 days, I put together a hearing in room 2172 of the Rayburn building as chairman of the Human Rights committee. We invited several people who gave compelling testimony that students and others were killed at Tiananmen Square—that he was a liar.

So we invited the Embassy to send somebody. We invited Chi Haotian to come. Obviously, we had an empty chair. We had that very prominently displayed.

But we had people from Time magazine, the People's Daily—a journalist who actually went to prison for trying to expose what was happening because he sided with the students—all tell their stories and some of the students themselves.

So Chi Haotian, in the light of all the glare here in Washington, DC, said nobody died at Tiananmen Square. A couple weeks ago I had another hearing on torture in China. There have been two horrific reports—horrific in terms of what they found—by the special rapporteur for torture in China.

This is the U.N. special rapporteur, and we had people at this hearing including one Tibetan Buddhist who told us how he sat in the tiger torture chair for 1 month and 22 days. Had a large picture of what it looked like and we've had Christians, Pentecostals, Falun Gong, and others all tell us how they had been subjected to this horrific torture chair.

It is only one of many tools—horrible tools used by the Chinese Government. Previously, 20 years before that, I had a hearing of six survivors of the Laogai including a Tibetan Buddhist monk, Palden Gyatso, who brought in the cattle prods that were used under his arms, on his genitals, in his mouth, and when he tried to get in through security here in the Rayburn building they stopped him.

I had to come down and escort him and he said this is what they do to us every single day. I have raised that issue with the Chinese Government in Beijing, in Shanghai, and here in the United States through hearings, through meetings, over and over again and they categorically deny that there is any torture, and that the torture chair—the tiger chair—does not exist.

On human trafficking I have written four major laws—the major law on human trafficking known as the Trafficking Victims Protection Act. China is a basketcase when it comes to labor trafficking and sex trafficking, a magnet in large part because of the missing girls, tens of millions of girls who don't exist because of gendercide—the direct killing through sex-selection abortion of the girl child—and that has led to a magnet effect of trafficking. Plus, they announced that they were getting rid of the Laogai system and it was another subterfuge because they didn't. They just transferred that whole process.

I chair the Congressional-Executive Commission on China as well. We were hopeful that this was real and durable. It was actually not real and durable. It was just a transfer of how they deal with this idea of reform through labor and it is just as egregious as it was before.

I could go on in every category of human rights. There is censorship. I held the hearings with Google, Microsoft, and Cisco sitting here under oath saying that they are not part of the censorship.

So if you put ''Tiananmen Square'' in what was then google.cn, you got wonderful pictures of happy tourists. If you put it into Google here in the United States you got pictures of tanks. So censorship is very real and I tried it a Beijing Internet cafe and I couldn't get my name. When I put in anything about torture I got Guantanamo and I got what the Japanese did, and it was horrible, to the Chinese during World War II.

But nothing about Manfred Nowak's report as the Special Rapporteur on torture, which was a scathing indictment of the Chinese's systematic use of torture against Falun Gong, against Christians, against Tibetan Buddhists, Uyghurs, and others.

So my question is about credibility. You mentioned in your testimony that Dr. Huang Jiefu spent time under house arrest.

Dr. LEE. That was Wang Haibo.

Mr. SMITH. Okay. So he was not under house—but he works for the government. He does work for the government. He's right hand to Xi Jinping. He was Deputy Health Minister. Was he not Deputy Health Minister? No, let me ask you. Was he Deputy Health Minister?

Mr. MATAS. That's the question—was he Deputy Health Minister.

Mr. SMITH. That is the first question. Is he aligned or part of the Government of China?

Dr. DELMONICO. Jiefu Huang has been part of the government, obviously.

Mr. SMITH. Has been. Okay.

Mr. GUTMANN. If I may just respond——

Mr. SMITH. No, let me finish it. Then I'll ask you.

Mr. GUTMANN. After you then, please.

Mr. SMITH. Please. Thank you.

He has been part of the government and he may be a very sincere upright very focused man and wants to get this right. But he works for a government that systematically says things don't happen.

Now, my question would be how do you independently verify? In a country that is closed as it is, I don't know if you have access to the military hospitals where this practice appears to have happened.

They won't allow teams to go into their prisons from the International Red Cross to look at prison conditions. They won't allow it. How do you independently verify that even though he may be very sincere that anything he says, zero foreign customers for organ trafficking in 2016, how do you independently verify that when there has been such a backdrop of terrible duplicity, lies, and deception on the part of the government? Trust and verify. How do you do it?

Dr. DELMONICO. I am not an apologist. I am not here to tell you not to worry. I am not here to verify. That is not my job.

My job is to say to you that the international community is trying to make change within China and work with those professionals that want to develop a system that conforms with the guiding principles of the World Health Organization and the Declaration of Istanbul.

That is my job. So let me say to you candidly I respect you greatly, Congressman Smith. I know of all the things that you recited for us this afternoon in your efforts. I have been in the midst of those for the last decade hearing the same things that you have heard.

The people of China said the very same things—we are not using the organs from the executed. They denied it. However, in this past decade, what has happened?

The state council no longer officially sanctions that practice. Whether it is going on or not, I can say to you that is a change.

I have met with the Minister of Health and said to her that if she wants China to ascend in the leadership of organ donation and transplantation in this world, they must stop the use of organs from the executed because there will be no presentations of such an experience in international fora or in the medical literature such as the New England Journal of Medicine or the transplantation literature. It won't happen, Madam Minister. It is not going to happen.

So I have been just as candid in my relationship with the Chinese as you have been, sir, and I am not here to verify or make credible.

I am here to say to you that there is a move within the country to change and the transplantation community recognizes what has been an abhorrent practice and was told that it wasn't happening.

Did not believe it and continued to work with the Chinese to make something different. In that regard, Jiefu Huang has indeed most recently been courageous, been at peril and the fight is going on even on this day as to who is going to succeed, whether the old system and the old guard will return to power or not.

Mr. SMITH. Could I ask you, are there zero cases of——

Dr. DELMONICO. I don't know that. Well, let me say this to you. I know about a month ago—and I get all of these anecdotes through the Declaration of Istanbul—a woman from Vancouver, Canada went to Tianjin and got herself a transplant.

So we do know that it is occurring still within China. But it is not my—it is not my job to say to you that it is eradicated or completely stopped.

Mr. SMITH. Could I ask you—and this is strongly for the record to know this—are there any—I wrote a letter to Dr.——

Dr. DELMONICO. You wrote a letter to Philip O'Connell. We responded to you. I responded to you.

Mr. SMITH. Did we get a response?

Dr. DELMONICO. Yes, you did. No, there is a letter there.

Mr. SMITH. This is 10 questions.

Dr. DELMONICO. Mr. Smith, there is a letter from the Transplantation Society and I wrote to you as well personally, which we got no response—which we got no response.

Mr. SMITH. Well, we will respond to you.

Dr. DELMONICO. Thank you.

Mr. SMITH. Before we move on to the second round, with regard to the military hospitals—People's Liberation Army Hospital—do you have any access to that, those hospitals?

Dr. DELMONICO. No. I don't have access.

Mr. SMITH. So we have no idea. I mean, that is where many of these—I mean——

Dr. DELMONICO. Sure, it could be going on there.

Mr. SMITH. Okay.

Dr. DELMONICO. I cannot assure you of that. What I can assure is that the young people that are going to be the future transplant people of the country they are not in tune with that practice any longer. I have met them. I have been with them.

Now, I recognize Mr. Gutmann is going to say this is anecdotal and et cetera.

Mr. GUTMANN. I love anecdotes.

Dr. DELMONICO. No, no. But I can only present to you—Mr. Smith, I can only present to you my experience, right, and say to you that we are trying to change it.

Mr. SMITH. I don't question your motives. In fact, you want to change it and you're part of the agent of reform. The concern is no one does duplicity better than the Chinese Communist Party and I gave you just a few examples and, again, when I had my hearing 20 years ago it was the military that was part of this process and security guards and we vetted the guard that came and gave this testimony, we protected his identity big time. He ended up getting asylum here, and Harry Wu helped to facilitate all of that, the great human rights leader.

But, frankly, when I read the documentation it was overwhelming and the military was up to its gills in making money through this.

Mr. ROHRABACHER. If the other witnesses have a comment?

Dr. LEE. Yes, can I have one.

Mr. ROHRABACHER. Then go for a second round? Everybody can have—everybody can have a comment. So we will start with Mr. Lee.

Dr. LEE. Yes. Okay. Thank you, Chairman.

We have heard that Dr. Delmonico talked about the organ trafficking and it is not limited in China. It is also happening in India, Egypt, within other countries as well. And also the Congress has introduced the H.R. 3694 regarding the organ trafficking.

What I wanted to say is that in China the problem is much bigger than the organ trafficking and the numbers of these transplantation operations much bigger than the executed prisoners can be explained because if you look at the history between 1995 and 1990, executed prisoners is about 1,600 or 1,700 a year. Then after the persecution of Falun Gongs, these numbers stays the same or even a little less.

However, the transplantation numbers exploded. So we have tons of evidence showing that the majority of these donors were Falun Gong practitioners. And also, this is not just organ trafficking for, like, organ——

Mr. ROHRABACHER. It is very, very clear what you're saying. There is evidence——

Dr. LEE. Yes, yes. But——

Mr. ROHRABACHER [continuing]. That the Falun Gong prisoners are a—there is a large—there is evidence to suggest they are way more representative than they are in the population in the number of donors supposedly that they are.

Dr. LEE. I think the point is that we cannot, like, shift the focus because what we are talking about is a state-sponsored crimes. It is organized by the Communist Party. It is not like the Mafia or some underground organized crime. This is like the entire country is organized—summoned to do these crimes, and you cannot compare this crime to any organ trafficking in other countries, even those also, you know, should be condemned and prevented.

So I think also for the communist regime to admit that they have been using executed prisoners it is not because they have found their conscience.

It is because the evidence about this harvesting of Falun Gong practitioners is too big and they cannot deny it so they can—they use the excuse of, you know, executed prisoners as kind of a lie, you know, to that they are not harvesting organs from a Falun Gong practitioner.

So this is—this must be made clear that we cannot just condemn organ trafficking instead of, you know, losing the big picture.

Mr. ROHRABACHER. Mr. Gutmann.

Mr. GUTMANN. What is the question exactly?

Mr. ROHRABACHER. Do you have a comment? And then we are going to go to a second round and then——

Mr. GUTMANN. Well, nothing really. I would just point out sort of, I guess, supporting Congressman Smith's point, I am holding this document. Actually, it was just given to me today but these kinds of things keep turning up. This is the China Red Cross and this is—it is on the eve of New Year's so 12/30/2015. This is the year that supposedly China went kosher and stopped harvesting any prisoners at all.

The voluntary donors go up in one single day from the 30th of December to the night of the 31st of December of 25,000 exactly—25,000 voluntary donors in a single day. That's the kind of thing that—you know, it is all very well to talk about—and I take your point about anecdotes because I write a lot of anecdotes too.

But, you know, when you start to sift through this kind of data this is the kind of thing you keep turning up. These numbers are fictional. They are flat out lies. This is a government that lies as it breathes.

So I think, you know, the point is I don't really agree with Dr. Delmonico that it is not at all their responsibility to do verification.

I do believe that, you know, Jeremy Chapman, he's—wait a second—Jeremy Chapman has a right to say anything he likes about us but he basically said we were completely—had no credibility whatsoever.

Mr. ROHRABACHER. Okay. You made your point and——

Mr. GUTMANN. We have a right to—you know, I think, you know, the point is we are supposed to be working together on trying to verify these issues.

Mr. ROHRABACHER. And Mr. Matas, do you have a comment? Your microphone is not on.

Mr. MATAS. Yes. I had a couple comments.

First of all, Representative Smith, I appreciate your—the context in which you put everything because I think this issue has to be approached contextually about what's generally happening in China now and in Chinese immediate history.

Dr. Delmonico and I were on a panel a month ago in Rome together and I'll repeat here what I said then, that it is impossible to have an island of respect for the rule of law and human rights in the transplant field in a raging sea of tyranny and dishonesty everywhere else in the system—that in order to get the transplant system to work you have to have respect for the rule of law and human rights generally.

That doesn't mean that the transplant profession is powerless and I think peer pressure is useful as leverage and it has worked in the past.

Two years ago, the Transplantation Society had their international conference here in the United States, San Francisco. They rejected 35 papers from China and they didn't go to an international conference in China to which they were invited 2 years ago and that had an impact in China.

This year, the Transplantation Society is meeting in Hong Kong. They haven't rejected the papers coming from China. Well, there certainly has been a lot more of them accepted and, again, than what happened 2 years ago. It hasn't been as systematic and I have looked and others have looked at the papers that are accepted and there is problems with those papers.

And the point is not to argue about which papers should be accepted or not but to point out that the transplantation can be—transplantation profession can be useful but in order to be useful in exercising peer pressure they have to develop the kind of contextual approach that you, Representative Smith, has presented—to know that there is lack of access, that there is bamboozlement, that there is denial, that there is dishonesty and be able—not to be too easily beguiled.

Mr. ROHRABACHER. To be fair, we are going to give you 30 seconds to answer the comments and then we'll go to the second round of questions.

Dr. DELMONICO. Transplantation is a noble act.

Mr. ROHRABACHER. What is that now?

Dr. DELMONICO. Transplant—organ donation and transplantation is a noble act. It has been my whole life and in all of our community it is a noble act. It is a giving of one person to another.

So when David says it is a human rights issue, it is a human rights issue. And why is that? Because it must be for the community to safeguard the well-being of the living donor and for us to make certain that organs that are recovering from the deceased are fairly justly distributed throughout the society.

So I completely agree with David's objectives of making this a human rights issue. It has been for the Transplantation Society and the World Health Organization of which I have representation and in this country to assure that. So please know of that.

Mr. ROHRABACHER. Okay. All right.

Dr. DELMONICO. Please know of it.

Mr. ROHRABACHER. All right. Thank you very much.

This is for a second round which we will try to make a little bit quicker. Let me just note when you have an operation on someone and you're cutting them open to cut out a piece of cancer, that is a noble act.

When you stick a bayonet in somebody and cut them open in order to suppress them or to create a feeling among a population that they are going to be—that you are now able to do a horrible thing like cutting somebody's head off like we see with ISIL, that is—okay, they are both cutting—they are both cutting somebody open.

And in this particular case what we are talking about is cutting somebody open, okay, and from what I have heard—just from what I have heard, the verification is coming from—and to be very fair to you, sir, you are basing your policies which you wanted policies on what will happen in the future after the era of reform that is going to take place in China.

And, frankly, I have been hearing about that for the last 25 years, longer than that—that there is going to be this nirvana in China if we keep treating them much more openly and we open up the communications with us, as long as we can talk to some of the young people there and give them some of the skills they need, which sometimes when they turn around are able to use to build weapons or to build things that actually repress their own people.

I have been hearing this for 25—we are going to have by just more interaction with them officially and telling them our expectations that they will be reformed.

I don't see the reform in China. I see them making a lot more money. I see them building better systems of repression. You were talking about the old gang returning. I am sorry.

I don't see the current gang to be so laudatory. We just—what have we talked about here, infanticide—you know, where we—babies have been killed and now they say that is only going to be—people can have two babies before they mass slaughter all the rest of them. There has been, of course, forced abortion and as we mentioned—or infanticide against people with—even if babies are born, if they are born with defects—am I wrong here—that in China today babies born with defects end up not getting home.

How about the fact that there are no labor unions. There are no opposition newspapers. There are no opposition parties. There are none of these things, and what there is is torture. What there is is all these evil things that we have noted and the nirvana that I have been promised all of these years and we, Congress, has been promised will happen because if we just engage with them and get them into our economy they are going to become more noble people and accept the values of what, I guess, the establishment that you're talking about is going to be very happy with them and being happy with the establishment is what will get them to change their behavior.

Dr. DELMONICO. Chairman, I am not—I am not here to promise you anything and I am not here to have a conclusion. All of the comments that you made about reprehensible activity is something that I condone.

Please, I want to make that clear in the record.

Mr. ROHRABACHER. Yes, sir.

Dr. DELMONICO. I don't condone any of that and I am not here to promise you anything and I am not here to assure you nirvana. I am only here to say that the international community has recognized this terrible practice in China and it wishes to change it and it has been asked to help to change it and instead of sitting on the sideline we are going there to develop an infrastructure of organ donation and transplantation that would be consistent with World Health Organization principles. That is my job. That is my job.

Mr. ROHRABACHER. Yes, and you——

Dr. DELMONICO. And I receive no funds for that, right. This isn't something which I am selling for.

Mr. ROHRABACHER. All I can tell you is setting up systems—setting up systems——

Dr. DELMONICO. They are trying to set up systems that you, sir, would——

Mr. ROHRABACHER [continuing]. In which—setting up systems in which a—in which you are one of the participants of the system is a Nazi.

You could expect that there would be some things coming out of that system that you don't like or the whole system will actually be perverted and used in a way that no one intended it to be used.

For example, today people can be lulled to sleep in the United States as we have been for 20 years, lulled to sleep in to thinking there is a fundamental change in China. It is coming, there is an era coming, we can work with them now. Their new generation is so much different.

I am sorry. I don't think the new generation is that much different in China today except maybe they are different from Mao and—but anyway, with that said I think that this is—thank you for—by the way, just thank the whole panel but thank you especially, Dr. Delmonico. You have been a real trooper to express your points of view here and I take it all in good faith and trust——

Dr. DELMONICO. Yes, let us all just sleep and we are working hard.

Mr. ROHRABACHER. All right. By the way, I get the same criticism when I am talking about trying to work with Russia to defeat radical Islam.

But you know what? There has been reform in Russia. There has been no opposition parties, no opposition papers—all of that stuff I just mentioned. A lot of that stuff has happened at least part way in Russia. In China, there is no—they haven't had any of that.

And also, you go to China and you notice that people, you know, there is an underground church movement there. But in Russia, they actually allow them now. They don't have to be an underground church in Russia.

(Off mic comments)

Well, I think that there has been some change in Russia and there hasn't been in China, and I think that is what it comes down to. And I think that the—it is the old thing. I say this all the time, for people who haven't heard it, is that the theory that if we treat them well and we let them into our markets and we increase their standard of living by allowing technology transfer and our marketplace is open that the people who run China and have been responsible for this infanticide and the forced abortions and all of these things that we are talking about here—organ transplants and then the rest—that those people will change their ways.

They will become decent people and you will now have—hugging them like they are liberals will change their heart. It won't, and I just—I call it the hug a Nazi, make a liberal theory and it just hasn't worked.

And that is why today I believe in we need to be tough, really tough on these issues instead of going about it just to be really cooperative with them and I think that is the essence of it.

Chris, would you like to take over?

Mr. SMITH. Thank you very much, Mr. Chairman.

I am glad Chairman Rohrabacher mentioned labor unions. Again, another example of the country of China with its state-run labor union, which is a farce, and no way comports with ILO standards. I have chaired hearings on that as well.

Our annual report looks at that, at the Congressional-Executive Commission on China, in great depth and there is no sense that—and I say that because there is right now an all-out effort by Xi Jinping and others who would love to be part of the TPP to somehow suggest that they will conform or are conforming now even to those standards.

I went and read the TPP. It leaves the enforcement mechanism to the country itself. So we would have to count on Chinese courts to say they do or do not have labor rights. There is no collective bargaining.

Arrearages is a problem. OSHA-type protections are nonexistent and, again, we get this big tsunami of disinformation out of China about they have a state labor union, but it is not protected.

So it is another example in a long series of examples of the context that Mr. Matas mentioned earlier, which I think is so important.

So maybe another question would be Dr. Wong Jiefu, how many others do you have—remember, he is a former—I don't know who pays his salary now because usually it is the government for something like this but maybe not——

Dr. DELMONICO. He's the head of a—can I mention——

Mr. SMITH. Yes.

Dr. DELMONICO. He's the head of a foundation that has received funding from a benefactor independent of China to now make—for the support for this change. So——

Mr. SMITH. Now, do you work with others too and could you name any of those individuals, any other docs?

Dr. DELMONICO. Oh, yes.

Mr. SMITH. Who you would believe can tell us, for example, what is going on in the military hospitals?

Dr. DELMONICO. I can't tell you about the military hospitals.

Mr. SMITH. Okay. But that is a big point that needs to be emphasized here because that is where we believe a lot of this is happening.

Dr. DELMONICO. Let us emphasize it together. I can't tell you about the military hospitals. That is fine.

Mr. SMITH. Okay. And maybe our other witnesses would want to elaborate on that.

You know, Xi Jinping, you know, this group that is supporting him and the foundation you mentioned has a draft NGO law that severs ties with——

Dr. DELMONICO. This is a foundation in organ donation and transplantation. It——

Mr. SMITH. But you are outside the country, right?

Dr. DELMONICO. No, no. It was a benefactor hotel magnate who supported this foundation.

Mr. SMITH. Is it a Chinese foundation or——

Dr. DELMONICO. It is a Chinese foundation, yes.

Mr. SMITH. Oh, it is in-country.

Dr. DELMONICO. It exists in Beijing but it is not a matter of the government and now Jiefu Huang is the head of that foundation and that is what supporting the infrastructure of developing organ procurement organizations similar to what we have in the United States.

I can't, again, guarantee this is going to happen. We have to try, however. We have to try.

Mr. SMITH. Let me just ask you, I did ask—and maybe through Mr. Gutmann and Mr. Matas—Dr. Jeremy Chapman, as we know the former president of the Transplantation Society, called the estimates in your report ''pure imagination piled upon political interest.''

I know because I work on human rights across the board around the world then when the B'nai Brith or the American Jewish Committee or some other organization dealing with Catholics or other, when we get information on Tibetan Buddhists we, obviously, try to do our due diligence and Congressmen and Senators to ensure that the information is accurate.

But to single out the Falun Gong and the others who are victims of this in the way—in such a dismissive way, I mean, it is beyond insulting. I wonder what you think of that dismissal of your work.

Mr. MATAS. Well, I am a litigation lawyer so I am used to people disagreeing with me. In fact, that is my daily fare. So and but, certainly, this is not a work of my imagination.

We, as I said, had in this report 2,400 footnotes. Everything we have done anybody can see. Every piece of evidence that we have looked at anybody else can look at. Anybody else who wants to look at it and has done the independent research has come to the same conclusion we had. In terms of political interest, I have none.

I am not—I did want to comment about what Representative Rohrabacher said earlier, which—I mean, obviously, I agree with everything you said but I did want to point out that this isn't a China problem. It is a communism problem.

This is the way communist—because I have been involved in human rights a lot of places around the world and I see this pattern behavior with the Soviet Union, with North Korea and so on. And, of course, the victims here are almost entirely if not entirely Chinese.

I mean, we, who are standing for the victims, are doing more—we are more pro-China, more standing up for China than the Communist Party of China is and——

Mr. ROHRABACHER. I am really happy that you brought that up because I, obviously, have taken some very tough stands against the Chinese Government and I just—our greatest ally in the fight to create a better world is—are the people of China.

And this is all—in fact, the motive here between Chris and myself, we are motivated by—we want to help the people of China. So thank you for making that distinction. We don't want anybody to think otherwise.

By the way, but about communism—you know, I have studied communism from the time I was a kid. I mean, I actually read Marx and Lenin and all these things. This is certainly not a Marxist government there. I mean, when you have—this is more like a fascist—a Leninist fascism.

But it is not—it is no longer the idea that they are going to create this new man, as Marx was suggesting, by ridding us of this profit motive and property rights to own things. But it is fascism of some kind.

Mr. MATAS. Well, and——

Mr. ROHRABACHER. But your point stands true. We are not—we are against these Chinese dictatorships and the Chinese people they are our greatest ally in making a more peaceful world.

Mr. MATAS. And my primary focus as a human rights advocate has been the victims, not the perpetrators. Those have to be our primary concern.

Mr. ROHRABACHER. Right. Right.

Mr. MATAS. You know, if Jeremy Chapman wants to insult me, I am not going to insult him back. I would just say look at our work. You don't have to—I don't care what people think of me. Just look at the stuff we have done.

Mr. SMITH. Let me ask you if I could, Dr. Delmonico, then Mr. Gutmann, if you wanted to comment as well.

You were chairman of the TTS, what, between 2012 to 2014?

Dr. DELMONICO. To the present.

Mr. SMITH. To the present? Okay. Has TTS ever requested evidence that sourcing organs for transplant from prisoners came from military hospitals and whether or not it has ceased?

Has that inquiry been made? Was it made under your watch? Has it been made since?

Dr. DELMONICO. I have gone to China and asked for a transparency of practice that is consistent with the World Health Organization principles.

That means that every transplant, every donor should be recorded. That's what our—that is what our policy is. So I have looked at the Minister of Health——

Mr. SMITH. I know, but did you ask the military——

Dr. DELMONICO. I have looked at the Minister of Health just like we are looking at each other right now, sir, and I have said to the Minister, we must have a transparency of practice that says recording of every single transplant with every donor to know——

Mr. SMITH. Did you get it?

Dr. DELMONICO. What we got was—what we got was in response that was unacceptable and upon that unacceptability of knowing that the practice was still continuing I wrote an open letter with Jeremy Chapman and other members of the international community, which I can submit to you, and it has been, it should be before you—an open letter to President Xi Jinping to stop the corrupt practice because just as you we were not at all satisfied with the response that we got and we said in that letter that until there was some move of transparency which now is under the COTR system—there is a China Organ Transplant Registry system that is now in place—there will be no presentation of papers or in the medical literature of the China experience, and that was our position statement.

Mr. SMITH. But there was no delineation or anything by way of response that was going on in the military. Here's another reason why I am stressing the military.

Xi Jinping and his crackdown on religion and this crackdown on NGOs—on religion NGOs now have to report to public security and not to what was a Communist Party apparatchik group before that.

So he has militarized it even further, and since that is an area where we have an absolute dearth of information—you don't know it, I don't know it, we don't know what's going on there—I think—does he even suggest that there might be zero or——

Dr. DELMONICO. That doesn't mean that I condone it.

Mr. SMITH. I know, but I think we have to insist on getting that and wonder why we are not getting the data. What are they hiding in the military hospitals?

Dr. DELMONICO. Agreed.

Mr. SMITH. Okay. Let me ask one final question, if I could, and this is, again, to just make sure this is absolutely on the record, are there any financial incentives or business dealings between individuals in the TTS leadership and mainland China's medical companies or any other mainland entities that could possibly create the appearance of a conflict of interest?

Dr. DELMONICO. I can only answer—my travel to China was supported—my travel to support—to go to China was paid for by the China Foundation.

Mr. SMITH. Is that a government foundation or not?

Dr. DELMONICO. It comes from—I am telling you that the foundation paid for my travel. That's who paid for the travel.

Mr. SMITH. But is that an entity of the Chinese Government?

Dr. DELMONICO. I am not aware that that is an entity of the Chinese Government. As I told you earlier, Mr. Smith, my understanding is that this foundation has been established by a benefactor who is a hotel magnate and that is how the foundation has been established.

And the objective is to develop infrastructure for organ procurement organizations within the country that would comply with WHO principles. That's what we are up to and that is the truth of it.

Mr. SMITH. Would anybody else like to go? And thank you, Dr. Delmonico.

Mr. MATAS. Well, I don't want to comment on his—he is answering for himself. But I want to comment on the fact that he is only answering for himself because——

Dr. DELMONICO. Well, it is not for me to answer for everybody else.

Mr. MATAS. Fair enough.

Mr. SMITH. When you were present.

Dr. DELMONICO. Well, during my—no, there was none. So if that—thank you for that question of clarification. There was none.

Mr. SMITH. We have asked that question in a letter that was dated on April 7th to Dr. O'Connell and we are awaiting that answer. Thank you.

Mr. ROHRABACHER. Well, I think this has been a good hearing and, again, let me first of all congratulate—you knew, Dr. Delmonico, you knew there would be—this would be—you would be in the hot seat and——

Dr. DELMONICO. I don't mind that. We are working hard to make some change.

Mr. ROHRABACHER. I know. I know you don't and that is why I am thanking you for coming today.

Dr. DELMONICO. Came here on my own—at my own cost.

Mr. ROHRABACHER. Yes. I have—again, I have had to withstand—I honestly believe that——

Dr. DELMONICO. China is not paying for me to be here today. Thank you.

Mr. ROHRABACHER. Yes. I actually believe that we need to have better relations with Russia and I was—I have always been a big enemy of the Soviet Union from the time I was a kid and I at times stand alone like you do and the secret is, however, we have to be scrupulously honest with each other and we have to trust each other's points of view.

But we need to express things and specifics and make sure that they make sense and that we as decision makers are getting a truthful view and an accurate view.

I don't think that we have had the reform in China that we were promised.

Dr. DELMONICO. I am not alone, though, Mr. Chairman. I am here with the World Health Organization as well.

Mr. ROHRABACHER. Sure. Well, all I can——

Dr. DELMONICO. That is not alone.

Mr. ROHRABACHER. Well, you know, all I can tell you is that when you talk about certain people in the establishment who want this and that I would just have to say that, for example, the people would like to say there is a difference between corrupt practices and official corrupt practices.

And in fact in places like China they are just meshed together because you have got an establishment. And again, it is not communism because these are millionaires.

These guys who are—the supposed communist bosses are millionaires and own hotels and things and they get involved in that way. They have their own little—they have their establishment.

Well, with that said, this is—what is important is that we have sent a message out that this issue, first of all, we have sent a lot of messages about China but in particular we have sent a message out that the issue of taking organs from a person who does not want to be a donor of an organ, especially if that person is a prisoner, especially if that person is a prisoner of conscience like the Falun Gong, that we are aware that that is happening in China today and that we are—we will not tolerate it and it is on our radar scope. That is what our message is today. Hopefully, that message will get in Beijing but also to other countries——

Dr. DELMONICO. India.

Mr. ROHRABACHER [continuing]. Where these things are happening.

Dr. DELMONICO. Mr. Smith, I hope you can include that in the TIP report. I hope that category can be—that is something I would ask you directly.

Mr. SMITH. If that legislation passes the Senate, it will.

Dr. DELMONICO. That is a reassuring comment. Thank you.

Mr. ROHRABACHER. All right. So with that, thank you, and Chris, I am going to give you the last——

Mr. SMITH. Oh, I think you have said it.

Mr. ROHRABACHER. Okay. There it is. Thank you all very much. This hearing is adjourned.

(Applause)

[Whereupon, at 3:46 p.m., the committee was adjourned.]

APPENDIX

SUBCOMMITTEE HEARING NOTICE
COMMITTEE ON FOREIGN AFFAIRS
U.S. HOUSE OF REPRESENTATIVES
WASHINGTON, DC 20515-6128

Subcommittee on Africa, Global Health, Global Human Rights, and International Organizations
Christopher Smith (R-NJ), Chairman

Subcommittee on Europe, Eurasia, and Emerging Threats (R-CA), Chairman

June 22, 2016

TO: MEMBERS OF THE COMMITTEE ON FOREIGN AFFAIRS

You are respectfully requested to attend an OPEN hearing of the Committee on Foreign Affairs, to be held by the Subcommittee on Europe, Eurasia, and Emerging Threats in Room 2172 of the Rayburn House Office Building (and available live on the Committee website at http://www.ForeignAffairs.house.gov):

DATE: Wednesday, June 23, 2016

TIME: 2:00 p.m.

SUBJECT: Organ Harvesting: An Examination of a Brutal Practice

WITNESS: Mr. David Matas
                  Senior Legal Counsel
                  B'nai Brith Canada

                  Mr. Ethan Gutmann
                  Journalist

                  Francis L. Delmonico, M.D
                  Professor of Surgery
                  Harvard Medical School

                  Charles Lee, M.D.
                  Director of Public Awareness
                  World Organization to Investigate the Persecution of Falun Gong

By Direction of the Chairman

The Committee on Foreign Affairs seeks to make its facilities accessible to persons with disabilities. If you are in need of special accommodations, please call 202/225-5021 at least four business days in advance of the event, whenever practicable. Questions with regard to special accommodations in general (including availability of Committee materials in alternative formats and assistive listening devices) may be directed to the Committee.

COMMITTEE ON FOREIGN AFFAIRS

MINUTES OF SUBCOMMITTEE ON _Europe, Eurasia, and Emerging Threats and Africa, Global Health, and Human Rights_ HEARING

Day __Thursday__ Date __June 23, 2016__ Room __2200 Rayburn__

Starting Time __2:00 pm__ Ending Time __3:46 pm__

Recesses | _0_ | (____to ____) (____to ____) (____to ____) (____to ____) (____to ____) (____to ____)

Presiding Member(s)

Rep. Rohrabacher

Check all of the following that apply:

Open Session ☑   Electronically Recorded (taped) ☑
Executive (closed) Session ☐   Stenographic Record ☑
Televised ☐

TITLE OF HEARING:

Organ Harvesting: An Examination of a Brutal Practice

SUBCOMMITTEE MEMBERS PRESENT:

Rep. Smith

NON-SUBCOMMITTEE MEMBERS PRESENT: _(Mark with an * if they are not members of full committee.)_

_N/A_

HEARING WITNESSES: Same as meeting notice attached? Yes ☑ No ☐
(If "no", please list below and include title, agency, department, or organization.)

STATEMENTS FOR THE RECORD: _(List any statements submitted for the record.)_

Several statements from Dr. Charles Lee

TIME SCHEDULED TO RECONVENE _____
or
TIME ADJOURNED ___3:46 pm___

_____
Subcommittee Staff Director

Statement for the Record

EE&ET/AGH Joint Subcommittee Hearing

June 9, 2016

My responsibility as a leader of the international community is to support the change that is underway in China from a reprehensible practice that used organs from the executed prisoner.

That support has been done through an alliance with Jiefu Huang, who is head of the China Organ Development Foundation and by the mission of the World Health Organization under the mandate of Resolutions of the World Health Assembly.

I consider Dr. Huang to be a courageous leader in the midst of what has been a corrupt practice. Dr. Huang states that "he as a transplant surgeon has never participated in the acquisition of organs from the executed prisoners and has desperately fought to make a difference for many years since return to China from Australia".

The China Organ Development Foundation has supported my visits to hospitals in China (by travel and lodging) where I have observed the transplantation of organs from patients who have died in the intensive care units of the hospitals I visited. These visits were done with a colleague from the World Health Organization and from the Donation and Transplant Institute (DTI) of Spain. The purpose of these visits (by my career experience) has also been for the development of infrastructure that would establish organ procurement organizations in China. The COTRS (China Organ Transplant Registry System) has been designed to achieve the equitable distribution of organs for a computerized waitlist of candidates – a national program that is consistent with WHO Guiding Principles and the Declaration of Istanbul. We have observed its application in multiple cities of China.

I received no honorarium or salary for those visits nor do I seek personal funding in the effort to bring change throughout China. The China Organ Development Foundation did not fund the travel and lodging for my testimony at the Congressional Hearings.

I acknowledge that the goal of a transparent practice of organ donation and transplantation in China is not completed. But neither is it completed in India or Egypt or Mexico. Organ trafficking and transplant tourism is a worldwide problem and has been experienced in the United States that led to the conviction of an individual in New Jersey.

The name of the hotel magnate that I have become aware as a benefactor for the China Organ Development Foundation --brought to attention in the Congressional hearings --is James Fox.

My experience in working with the China Organ Development Foundation has not been as an exercise for the Communist Party or the Government of China;
-- it has been by a collaboration with a current generation of transplant professionals in making change in the hospitals of China that I and the other international colleagues from the WHO and DTI and The Transplantation Society have visited.

It is to those professionals of China and the patients of China
and to the noble practice of organ donation and transplantation worldwide,
that we are committed.

Francis L. Delmonico, M.D.

World Health Organization
Advisory for Human Transplantation

Senior Advisor
Declaration of Istanbul Custodian Group
http://www.declarationofistanbul.org/

Professor of Surgery
Harvard Medical School
Massachusetts General Hospital Transplant Center

Chief Medical Officer
New England Organ Bank

NOTE: Material submitted for the hearing record by the witness Charles Lee, M.D., director of public awareness, World Organization to Investigate the Persecution of Falun Gong, is not reprinted here but is available on the Internet at: http://docs.house.gov/Committee/Calendar/ByEvent.aspx?EventID=105116

www.ingramcontent.com/pod-product-compliance
Lightning Source LLC
Chambersburg PA
CBHW081329310526
45789CB00018B/2727